THE
TWILIGHT
YEARS OF THE
EDINBURGH
TRAM

Volume 2 in a series of Twilight Years
(Volume 3 will cover Aberdeen and Dundee)

A.W. Brotchie

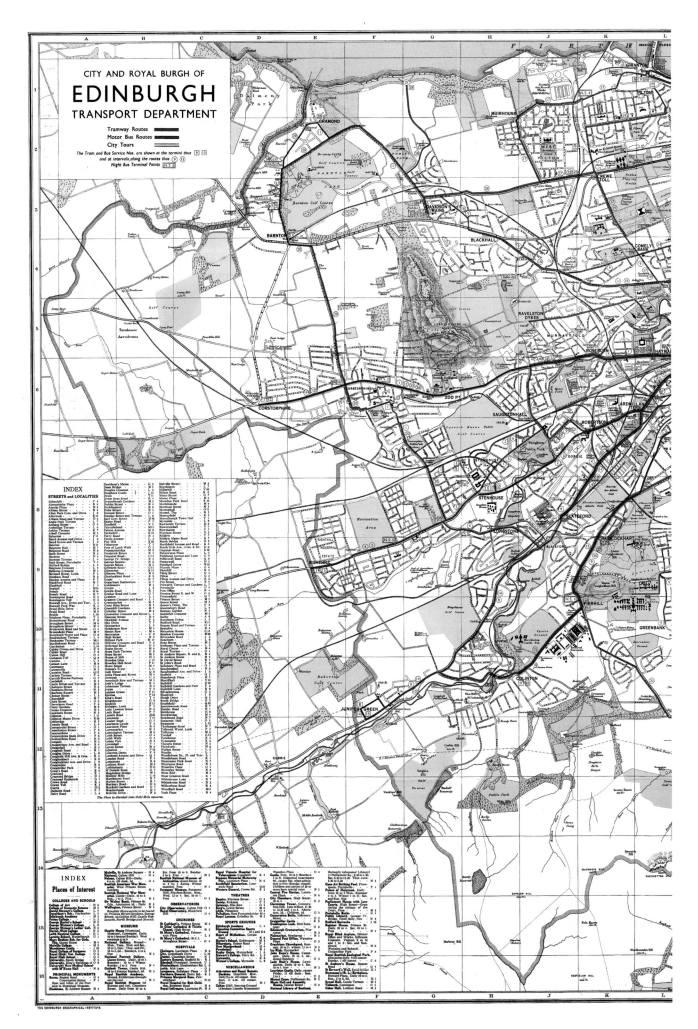

CITY AND ROYAL BURGH OF

EDINBURGH
TRANSPORT DEPARTMENT

Tramway Routes
Motor Bus Routes
City Tours

The Tram and Bus Service Nos. are shown at the termini thus ⑨ ⑮
and at intervals along the routes thus ⑨ ⑮
Night Bus Terminal Points N.S.⑦

THE EDINBURGH GEOGRAPHICAL INSTITUTE

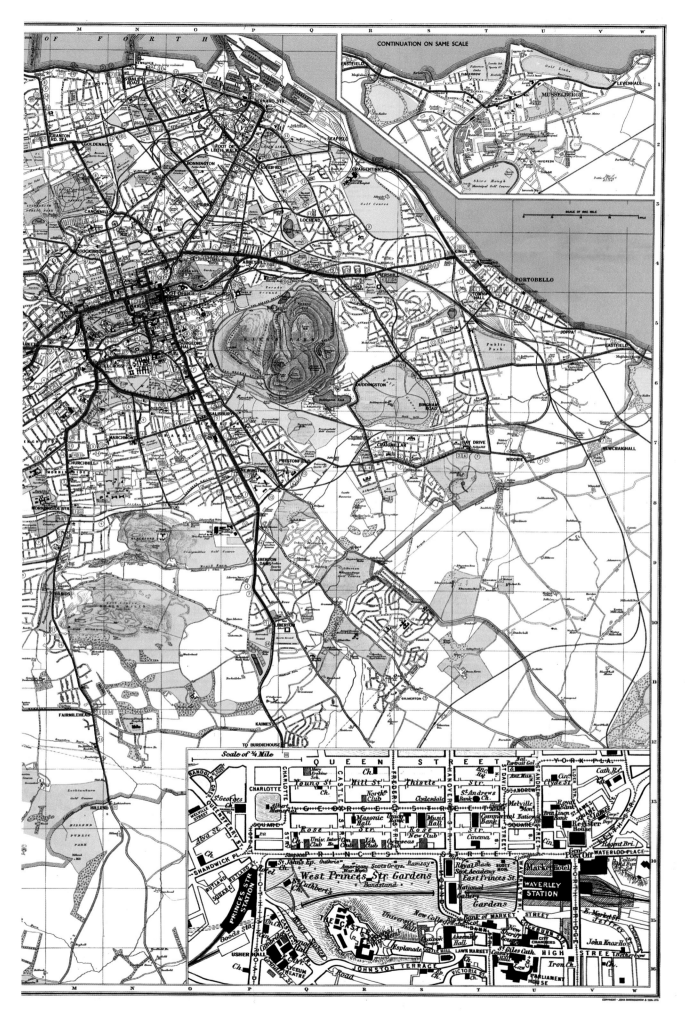

Copyright Notice

All rights in the text and illustrations are reserved; no part of these may, except under legislative allowance, be reproduced, stored in a retrieval system, or transmitted, in any form or by any means, electronic, mechanical, photocopying, recording or otherwise, without permission; copyright subsists as follows – text: A.W. Brotchie; illustrations: 2, 3, 16 – the late Allan Strachan; 1, 4, 5, 26, 73, 77, 82, 84, 111, 134, 179, 189 – late W.J.Wyse; 6, 8, 9, 10, 76, 78-80, 86 – C.Carter; 7, 11, 17, 22, 23, 25, 30, 31, 34, 36 – R.J.Braun; 15, 33, 130, 170 – publisher; 18, 19, 24, 27, 39, 81, 83, 94-99, 107, 116, 118, 121-123, 128, 133 – F.W.Hunt; 20, 126, 129, 169 – J.Copland, courtesy M.Jenkins; 40, 44, 109, 119, 124, 125, 135, 154, 158, 195 – Photobus/ J.Copland; 45, 46, 58, 60, 62, 64 – late R.B.Parr; 47, 48, 59, 61, 63, 66-72, 74, 75 – R.J.S.Wiseman; 49, 50-53, 57, 65, 127, 147, 148, 150, 151, 162, 164, 167, 171, 172, 174, 177, 178, 182, 187, 188 – M.J.Robertson; 54 – R.W.A.Jones; 55, 56 – M.G.C.Wheeler; 87, 88, 117, 120, 136-140, 144, 180, 191 – A.W.Brotchie Collection; 89, 91, 93, 105, 113, 114, 141, 142 – P.D.Hancock; 90, 92, 106, 156, 163, 166, 168, 184 – National Tramway Museum/M.O'Connor; 103, 104 – W.G.S.Hyde; 143 – Dr.S.J.T.Robertson; 145 – R.L.Grieves; 146 – N.D.G.Mackenzie; 149, 155, 157, 160, 165, 175, 181, 183, 186, 190, 192 – G.G.Fairley; 161 – A.D.Packer; 108, 193, 194 – A.G.Gunn. φ12, ♣13, 14, ♦35 – T.J.Edgington/Colour-Rail/φIR162/♣IR163/♦IR161; 21, 28, 29, φ37, ♣38, ♦42, ♥43, 110, 112, ♠115 – C.Banks collection/Colour-Rail/φIR232/♣IR230/ ♦IR231/♥IR233 /♠IR234; 32 – J.T.Inglis/Colour-Rail; 41, 85, 100, 176, 185 – Colour-Rail; φ101, 102, 131, ♣132, ♦153 – I.Davidson/Colour-Rail/φIR416/ ♣IR417/♦IR415; 152 – K.Bannister/Colour-Rail; 159, 173 – T.Marsh/Colour-Rail. Symbols refer to Colour-Rail catalogue reference numbers. Photographs by F.W.Hunt and the late W.J.Wyse are from the collection held by the Light Rail Transit Association, London Area.

Further acknowledgments by Alan W. Brotchie:
Thanks are due to all the above persons/bodies/estates, also: The City of Edinburgh Archivists Department, Charles Bilette, G.Hartley, M. Jenkins, M.A.Bridges MacWhirter, K.S.Mason, N.Renilson, Bill Roberton, A.Simpson, H.Stevenson, I.G.McM.Stewart, Prof I.Wooton, and lastly but not least my loving and long-suffering wife, June Anne.

Despite all reasonable efforts having been made, it has not been possible to determine the provenance of one or two of the photographs – any such are included under A.W.Brotchie Collection.

A catalogue entry for this book is available from the British Library

ISBN: 187442232X

Publication no.34

Published by Adam Gordon, Priory Cottage, Chetwode, Buckingham, MK18 4LB
Tel:01280 848650

Printed by Drogher Press, Unit 4, Airfield Way, Christchurch, Dorset, BH23 3TB

Typesetting by Trevor Preece, Gawcott, Buckingham

INTRODUCTION

The intention of this volume is to provide a companion to Adam Gordon's highly acclaimed 'Twilight Years of the Glasgow Tram', and to illustrate in mainly colour photographs the final years of the once ubiquitous and still fondly remembered Edinburgh tramway system. The compiler of that book had use of the large collection of colour views photographed by the late W.D.McMillan, but the Glasgow system closed in 1962, six years after that of Edinburgh. In these six years colour photography had progressed significantly, both in technical standards and in reduction of cost. Thus there is unfortunately no similar treasure trove of colour photographs, shot by one person, of fundamentally consistent quality and covering the varying geographic and distinctive features of the Edinburgh system.

The collections of as many photographers as possible have been accessed to produce the best selection of colour scenes of Edinburgh's trams. Visiting enthusiasts to the Capital City, in the few years between the intimation of the abandonment programme and its fulfilment had, in most cases, the laudable aim of recording details of the vehicle rather than the tram in its surroundings. As many views are therefore of the tramcar as a vehicle, this collection is divided into two main sections, geographical and vehicular. The non-enthusiast may consider there to be a certain amount of repetition, but it is felt that the record should be made as complete as possible.

The selection is the best of what has been made available – there are at least a further three dozen colour views of Edinburgh trams which for a variety of reasons have not been included. Generally these are very similar to those used. Thanks must be recorded to all the photographers who have generously allowed their historic negatives and slides to be used.

The general plan in the geographical section is to deal firstly with the city centre, then to work round the city, from northwest, in a generally anti-clockwise direction. To ensure as complete coverage as possible, some locations have – because no colour scenes have been found – been represented in black and white. These historic views, it is considered, justify their inclusion where, to omit them, would have created gaps in the coverage. Needless to say, it has not been possible to cover all situations or locations desired – if only a time machine was available to return to the 1950's to record all the scenes one now has only committed to memory...

An opportunity has been taken to illustrate the unique Edinburgh service colour light scheme. By means of two coloured lights below the service number the route of the car could be determined at night from a considerable distance. There was, when the scheme was introduced in 1922, a definite logic (although how many people actually knew that is open to question). For the record, a green light indicated a car going by way of Churchhill, red was for the Bridges, blue for Haymarket, yellow for Leith/Granton, and white for other areas. The original service pattern was however occasionally varied, but the colours were not altered. Some routes, such as those passing Portobello, did not follow this logic. The three routes heading east from Waterloo Place were red/red, green/green and blue/blue for Joppa, Levenhall and Port Seton respectively. The colour lights were a distinctive feature of Edinburgh's trams and a boon to travellers.

While not truly featuring in the tramway 'twilight', the opportunity has been seized to include appendixes on Edinburgh's cable and horse trams. The drawings of the varied liveries carried by the horse cars, by an unknown contemporary hand, are included for their historical value. While of a 'naïve' nature, they do portray the cars and their varied colours with accuracy.

Edinburgh's trams were an inescapable indicator of the City persona. Princes Street was a constant procession of madder (maroon) and white vehicles; most travellers to the City had their first sight of the trams as they emerged from Waverley Station on to Princes Street (described by Professor Charles McKean as an "architectural fruit salad"), but with its undisputed unique atmosphere.

Today's deregulated buses do not satisfy this writer. Competition may be necessary at some time, but when Corporations exercised legislated power to control competition within the City Boundary, any other services operating over the same streets as the Corporation vehicles had to charge fares in excess of the Corporation fares, and were prohibited from uplifting passengers on routes in the city. Such powers

5

gave protection to the Corporation's investment. These powers no longer exist. Major capital investment in power stations, electricity distribution networks, track and vehicles was dissipated with unseemly haste.

Fortunately – in terms of the public good – the wheel has turned full circle, and tramways (or to give their current title 'Light Rail Systems') are now seen as a highly desirable part of passenger transport, and reintroduction to Scotland's capital is being given serious consideration. The major stumbling block is the cost of replacing the infrastructure ripped out fifty years ago. While it has been found possible to reintroduce trams to several English centres (the latest being Croydon), differences between England and Scotland result in a lack here of the ability to achieve Government financial backing.

There must therefore be found a method of breaking this impasse. Edinburgh is one of the very few Capital cities of Europe relying solely on the diesel engine for local transport propulsion. To remove pollution from the atmosphere and improve air quality for all its citizens and the many visitors who enjoy the City and its environs, must be an imperative for both the Scottish Parliament and the City of Edinburgh Council. This is much too important to be a political football, and cross party support is needed to ensure that Scotland's capital has a quality public transport system which will attract people away from their cars.

CITY and ROYAL BURGH OF EDINBURGH TRANSPORT DEPARTMENT

NOTICE TO PASSENGERS

UNCOLLECTED FARES BOX

Passengers who have not had an opportunity of tendering their Fare to the Conductor are requested, before alighting, to place their Fare in the BOX provided on this Vehicle.

2 St James' Square
EDINBURGH, 1
March, 1944.

ROBERT M'LEOD,
Transport Manager.

Warwick & Sons Ltd., Edinburgh & Portobello.

EDINBURGH TRAMWAY 'HERALDRY'

Over the years Edinburgh Tramways, whether horse, cable or electric, have carried only five differing 'devices' to indicate their owners. It is extremely fortunate that examples of four from the five are still preserved.

When the Edinburgh Street Tramway Company commenced operation in November 1871, its cars carried a 'device' which it is thought was unchanged throughout its existence. Through the good offices of Mr G. Hartley we are able to illustrate this, the first of Edinburgh's tram insignia. A gold coloured garter carrying the Company title encloses two 'shields', on the left a stylised castle and on the right a blue coloured representation of a horse tramcar. The badge remained in use until 1904 when the Company was dissolved.

The Edinburgh Northern Tramways had a crest with a circlet of varying colour enclosing three or four shields; one with the recurring castle theme, another possibly a cable tram. No existing example of this device has been uncovered, and such monochrome illustrations as exist are not of reproducible quality.

When the Edinburgh & District Tramways Company took the lease of most of the horse tramways in 1894 their badge was then applied to the vehicles acquired. It was, as shown in the illustration, a colourful

representation of two of the city centre features, Castle and National Gallery, and was also later used on their cable trams.

Leith Corporation, when they took over the existing horse tramcars, did not bother to repaint them, so far as is known. However when their new electric trams were delivered they carried a representation of the Burgh seal and motto, as shown here. The seal shows a stylised sailing ship with the Virgin Mary and Christ Child. The significance of the cloud has not been explained.

On the Corporation takeover of tramway operation on 1 July 1919, the District crest was immediately painted out and replaced by the

(G. Hartley)

Coat of Arms of the City of Edinburgh – as reproduced opposite. This was carried on trams and buses until responsibility for local transport passed to Lothian Region from 16 May 1975. The coat of arms has been described "Argent, a castle, triple-towered and embattled sable, massoned of the first and topped with three fans, gules; windows and portcullis shut of the last; situated on a rock proper; supported on the dexter by a maid richly attired, with her hair hanging down on her shoulders, and on the left by a stag or deer proper; set on a wreath of the colours for the crest an anchor wreathed with a cable all proper". The application of the City coat of arms seemed to give the vehicles an undeniable place in the proper order of things.

2. The archetypal tourists' view from Edinburgh Castle across Princes Street Gardens – the valley of the former Nor' Loch – to Princes Street and the New Town, and beyond the northern suburbs to the River Forth and Fife c.1950. From this distance Princes Street appears with a constant procession of cost effective, electric, public transport. West of Castle Street were to be found many well remembered "institutions" – Spark's, Allan's, Fuller's cafe, Darling's and the Monseigneur News Cinema.

3. Looking north-east from the Castle's Forewall Battery across the Ross Bandstand (now officially the Ross Theatre) to the north side of Princes Street, and on the right Frederick Street – still with tram lines. The original 1790's house fronts of the east side of Frederick Street remain to this day largely unaltered, although the shop fronts have changed greatly. On this part of Princes Street the architecture has not altered, but of the 1950's retail outlets not one remains: Smalls, Mackies, Timpson and Etam are all gone; only the Overseas League Club retains its prime location. The sunshades are seldom seen – even on sunny days – over today's shop fronts.

4. Classic buildings and classic trams well portrayed in these 1951 scenes at one of Edinburgh's tramway nuclei in front of General Register House at the east end of Princes Street. This was a major interchange, with many routes coming up Leith Street (on the left), and others approaching from the Bridges and Princes Street to the right. Traffic appears able to cope with resurfacing operations (relaying the whinstone setts) without too much problem. Streamline car 13 is on service 11 from Stanley Road to Fairmilehead on this sunny, summer evening.

5. The same locus, the same time, but the constant procession of trams has changed; car 345 is en route to Colinton. Traffic movement here was so intense that the control of tramway points was in the hands of a pointsman ensconced in a tiny box in front of the Wellington Statue, behind the photographer. The Ionic porticos flanking both sides of the approach to Waterloo Place were created in 1815, part of the grand design to improve the eastern approach to Princes Street and form a proper statement to the start of the newly engineered road to London (Regent Road, designed by Robert Stevenson). The driver awaits a signal to move into Princes Street while the car behind is on service 8 to Newington Station.

6. At the top of Edinburgh's famously windy Waverley steps car 269 heads west on service 1 to Corstorphine. This was always a busy stop, with many passengers making for here immediately on leaving Waverley station. For a capital city, the interchange of passengers between rail, country bus and city transport has never been particularly well provided. A proposal to utilise the long disused Scotland Street tunnel to create a pedestrian link from Waverley to the reconstructed bus station is now being aired, but may be too radical for Edinburgh to adopt.

7. Crossing Princes Street could be done with poise and impunity in the fifties. Ankle socks, jaunty 'Tammy' and nylon raincoat all date the scene. Car 49 is headed east for Colinton on service 9; 234 on the left is on the outer, clockwise, Marchmont Circle, service 6. On the left 'gap' site the *Palace* Cinema formerly stood, demolished to allow an extension to Woolworth's store. The cinema, opened in 1913, had a frontage memorable for its white Sicilian marble columns (seen in the view above). It closed in February 1955, its final screening being 'On the Waterfront' starring Marlon Brando.

8. Heading east along the eastern half of Princes Street in the early 'fifties, car 28 is on service 11 to Stanley Road in Pilrig Street. The regulator standing beside the platform of the car will use his point lever to change by hand the points leading to South St. Andrew Street. These were not automatically controlled, but most junctions throughout the system were.

9. The same locus with a car on Marchmont Circle service 6 which will go ahead as far as the G.P.O. junction, then turn right to head south by way of the North and South Bridges. Summer white top caps are in evidence – but the driver's attention is being distracted by something. R. W. Forsyth, an Edinburgh institution for men's outfitting and rugby 'colours', built its distinctive Princes Street shop in 1906 but to the surprise and regret of many it closed in 1984.

10. Also photographed in front of the Forsyth store, car 48, on service 10 heading to Bernard Street, is less than one year in service. To most observers there were two obvious varieties of this type of car, pre-war as seen at the foot of page 14, with half drop top deck windows, and the later, with quarter drop top deck windows and ventilation louvres in the roof ends. Note also the much lighter colour of the window pillars and the panel above the lower window.

11. A sunny day view from the Scott Monument provides an unusual angle of tram 35, the ultimate choice as Edinburgh Corporation's museum piece. The tidy lines of the design are evident even from this angle. Photographed on a Saturday afternoon, to judge by Jenner's closed gates, but with crowds of shoppers still evident. The asphalt patch repairs to the granite sett paving were done in the knowledge that the whole street was soon to be completely resurfaced.

12. Car 257 loading westbound at the passenger island at the Scott Monument, Princes Street. It is on service 9 to Colinton, a 10-minute basic frequency service from Granton via Broughton Street. Behind is the 1883 bulk of the Old Waverley Hotel. At eight storeys it was when built the tallest building on the north side of the street.

13. The first 'streamline' design car, 262, is less than two years younger than 257 above, but represents a great move forward in tram design – Edinburgh's streamlined cars with (initially) bucket-type revolving seating were seen as something special. It is said that the design was influenced by similar cars built for Johannesburg tramways. Car 28 in front is from a later batch with a differing position for the route number box. A warm day, to judge by the 'shirt sleeve order'.

14. Loading from the passenger island is car 223 in July 1955. It is heading for Fairmilehead on route 11 from Stanley Road via Pilrig Street and Leith Street. Built in March 1939, it was always a Leith Depot car. A busy scene at the junction of Princes Street and South St. David Street.

15. Sunday morning scene, empty streets and drawn blinds. Car 238 on service 6 follows a similar car. Jenner's store displays its Royal Warrant granted for furnishings. The store is, with American Express, the only Princes Street retailer remaining in the same ownership to this day, very much an Edinburgh 'institution.' Founded as Kennington and Jenner in 1838, the name change took place thirty years later. The building dates from 1893, much being made of its 'fire-proof' construction – its predecessor having just burnt down! Its design is supposed to resemble that of the Bodleian Library in Oxford.

16. The east end of Princes Street is dominated by the Victorian "gothic rocket ship" erected 1840-6 in memory of Sir Walter Scott, photographed from St. Giles Street at the top of 'The News' steps. Trams rumble past his unblinking gaze, while his back is set against the bustle, smoke and steam of Waverley station. The soot-encrusted Binny sandstone of the monument contrasts with the white Carrara marble of the great man's statue. In the foreground, one of the (then) fifty year-old tank locomotives kept in immaculate condition for shunting duties. Formerly bright green, under British Railways they were repainted black, but remained in pristine state.

17. Looking east from the topmost balcony of the Scott Monument in the summer of 1955. Trams and buses in equal numbers where just a year previously trams had a monopoly of all these busy routes. In the distance the Firth of Forth, while closer to the camera, on the far left, is the dome of Register House, in the mid distance Calton Hill, its Royal Observatory and Edinburgh's Disgrace, then the tower of the North British Hotel – before its make-over to the 'Balmoral'. Note the clock – always two minutes ahead – for the 'benefit' of tardy train travellers.

18. Major changes under way in March 1956. Viewed looking to the foot of Hanover Street with car 195 heading east. Demolition is nearing completion of the old Royal Hotel, which will shortly be replaced by the first Edinburgh store of Messrs Marks and Spencer, with the new Mount Royal Hotel above. Behind the tram scaffolding precedes further demolition, on this occasion for the British Home Stores development.

19. Foot of the Mound junction from the steps of the Royal Scottish Academy also in the Spring of 1956. All eastbound vehicular traffic had to run by way of George Street during carriageway reconstruction, hence extra trams were run (as 'outer circle' 6's) to compensate for the absence of buses. The 1834 facade of the 'New Club' is prominent on the north side of the street. It was demolished in 1966 – one of the most missed of the hotchpotch of buildings which gave Princes Street its unique atmosphere.

20. Car 227, with not another east bound tram in sight – a major change from the scenes of just a year earlier. To the right a mix of small shops, best remembered perhaps being Austin Reed and John Sinclair's tobacconist, above them the Balmoral Restaurant.

21. Car 260 has, apparently, exclusive use of the east-bound track in this scene looking west to the foot of Frederick Street. Probably the best remembered from this clutch of shops is that of R. Marcus Ltd, furriers, at number 97, with its trio of stuffed bears visible in this scene with their flag poles, at first floor balcony level. Taken from the island seen in the view above.

22. Again a surprising lack of west bound trams, with empty tracks stretching into the distance. Young lads move to board car 89 on Marchmont circular route 6 – possibly the rolled towels under their arms indicate they are heading for Portobello Pool and will therefore need to change cars at the GPO.

23. Car 45 on the service 13 'circle' heading for Churchhill, with red white and blue pennants flying from the car's trolley rope – an Edinburgh Festival 'decoration'. Note the bus on tram replacement service 4. It was one of sixteen ten-year-old Daimlers which were modernised in 1954 for use on the first phase of the bus replacement programme. They only lasted till 1967. Behind is Small's drapery and furnishing store.

24. In the spring of 1956 car 91 approaches a tram island which is also being used as a temporary bus stop. The Leyland is one of the first batch of one hundred purchased in 1954 for operation of former tram routes. Behind the bus is the tearoom and bakery shop of J.W. Mackie and Sons. The coffee shop was then one of the few non-licensed establishments open of an Edinburgh evening.

25. Car 85 has only some 6 months left in service as it heads west on the 'inner' anti-clockwise service 6 Marchmont Circular. It was not often that these older cars were used on the 6 – whenever possible Tollcross depot would put out the later standard car. Note the bus stop and queue on the footpath – this was said to offer much safer loading than the tram islands in the middle of the street.

26. Major track reconstruction was undertaken in 1951 on Princes Street, before any decisions had been made on the super hasty abandonment plans. Car 151 of 1924 (formerly numbered 28) heads west to Stenhouse on service 3. At this time no less than sixteen tram services used all, or part of, Princes St. To the left is the shoe shop of James Allan & Son Ltd – which had a high-tech (!) x-ray machine to ensure that school-shoes had plenty of space in them for 'growth'.

27. Near the Castle Street junction with Princes Street with car 260 heading west. On the right is Darling's ladies' outfitters – another of Edinburgh's premier stores now only a memory. The name, however, is well remembered in the city, as proprietor Sir Will Y. Darling was the City's Lord Provost 1941-4, then went on to become the Conservative MP for the Edinburgh South constituency from 1945-57. The store site is now the Virgin Megastore, while Moffat the Photographer has given way to Laura Ashley.

28. Busier scene at the same locus, in July 1955. In addition to Darling and Moffat, the scene also includes a Thomas Cook travel agency – in those days overseas travel was reserved for the seriously well off – or so it appeared. Foreign tourists were few and far between in Scotland – the days of 'doing' off-season Edinburgh in February's rain and sleet were yet to dawn.

29. The same pink Austin A30 is outside Darlings – an impossible achievement today – with no private cars allowed to travel eastwards; only public service vehicles, taxis and bicycles. No such restrictions in the fifties. Three Edinburgh ladies allow car 21 heading for Colinton to pass by. Note its yellow 'Via Leith Walk' board.

30. Car 80 at the east-going passenger loading island on Princes Street at South Charlotte Street in August 1955. It only ran for a further three months before being scrapped. The attention of the smartly dressed lady seems to be gripped by the Corporation bus driver on his moped with his haversack for flask and sandwich slung carefully over his shoulder.

31. Car 76 heading west for Colinton on service 9 which succumbed to the bus on 23 October 1955 just a few weeks after the photograph was taken. On the left the brown marble shop front of the Macvittie, Guest & Co's shop and tearoom. (Source of still remembered fancy cakes consumed sitting on high wooden stools at the rear of the shop.) Another local company now just a memory.

32. Returning to the Hanover Street/Mound crossing, car 204 negotiates the point work. Flags flying from shops, and pennants on the tram's trolley rope all suggest the view dates from Festival time, August 1955. In those days ladies had to be careful crossing the streets as high heels could – and not infrequently did – get stuck in the tram rail grooves with disastrous results! Note the popular restaurant – the Brown Derby – above the Richard Shops' establishment.

33. The road sign, bottom left, tells us this is the Spring of 1956, when reconstruction of the Princes Street carriageway on either side of the remaining tram rails was undertaken. It is also fairly safe to assume that this is a Sunday morning, to judge from the lack of pedestrians. Car 111, a former Portobello Depot stalwart, is now working from Tollcross Depot on service 23. (This tram provided the number box for the illustrations in this book showing the service colours – with the greatest wear at '5'.)

34. Car 103 squeals round the reverse curves on its twisting crossing from Hanover Street, across Princes Street, to the Mound. Originally a pointsman operated both sets of points by hand. From the early fifties operation was automatic, with cars from North or South setting the points appropriately, resetting being achieved when the trolleyhead activated a skate on the overhead.

35. Pausing at the stop of the foot of the Mound, car 103 again basks in the western sun, casting long shadows. Note the flower baskets hanging between the pillars of the Royal Scottish Academy and the relaxed summer ambience that gave time to sit on the steps and watch the world go by.

36. The (Earthen) Mound, viewed from Edinburgh Castle. It was reputed to have consumed some two million cartloads of soil dumped from construction of the New Town with the roadway laid out in 1834-35. The railway followed in 1846 and the composition was completed by construction of the William Playfair designed National Gallery building of the late 1840's. The 14 acre glass roof of Waverley Station fills what was the Nor' Loch with the NB Hotel clock tower and behind the monumental confections of Calton Hill.

37. What is it about this tram descending the Mound that has so captivated these youngsters? More long shadows, but shown to good advantage are the silver and black traction poles that graced the city centre. Nobody seems to know what the rule was as to which were painted thus rather than the standard dark and mid green. Certainly Princes Street, George Street and the immediate environs of the City Centre were, as was the Mound and North Bridge; Regent Road changed to green at the Royal High School.

38. Car 69 ascends the Mound on route 27 to Craiglockhart in the late summer of 1955. Little did Edinburgh's citizens realise that, just forty four years later the General Assembly Hall behind New College at the top of the Mound would be the first – albeit temporary – home of the devolved Scottish Parliament.

39. Quiet scene (a Sunday?) as 220 comes cautiously down the Mound. On the left are the posts erected in 1924 at Board of Trade insistence prior to certifying that the electrified line could be re-opened for passenger traffic. They were installed to prevent any de-railed tram from careering down into the gardens and railway below. Still in place, they were never called into use during the tramway era.

40. Photographed from the same spot as the view above, the photographer having turned 90 degrees to his right, car 83 approaches the right-angled bend at the mid-point of its descent of the Mound. Behind the car hides the Bank of Scotland headquarters, but to the right is the striking Black Watch South African War Memorial, a kilted bronze warrior seemingly attentive to the defence of Scotland's temporary Parliament Building.

41. At the north end of Lothian Road, where it joins Princes Street's West End, car 253 on Granton Circular service 14 waits behind standard car on service 6. Across on the other side of the street is Binns Ltd (now Frasers) a 1930's replacement for the earlier Maules building. Many of Edinburgh services ran (when on timetable) to a specific order; for example 5s from London Road waited until the 7 coming up from Leith Walk passed, then fell into place behind it – a similar arrangement prevailing at the Salisbury Place junction.

42. In Lothian Road car 112 on service 9 follows an older car on service 6. Behind is the red Dumfriesshire sandstone bulk of the five-star Caledonian Hotel (which has not abdicated from its historic name – although it now trades as the Caledonian Hilton). As the ground floor was constructed some ten years in advance of the upper floors, a difference in stone texture and colour became visible after stone cleaning, but is now less apparent.

43. Heading for Fairmilehead on service 11, car 218 waits to allow passengers to board from the island at the foot of Lothian Road. To enable drivers to stop at precisely the head of the queue, there was a white indicator mark between the tracks for position. From here to Churchhill there was a choice of five services each with at worst a basic 10-minute frequency, a car every 2 minutes. Add to this the services which branched off at Tollcross, and some idea can be obtained of the facility provided.

44. Car 160 also seen at the foot of Lothian Road looking north with, behind, the Episcopal church of St John the Evangelist, dating from 1817, which is supposedly modelled on St. George's Chapel, Windsor. On Princes Street can be seen the facade of one of the city centre's many bank branches, this the granite face of the former British Linen Bank which has become a branch of Boots the Chemist.

45. For a time only trams were allowed passage between Shandwick Place and Hope Street – all other traffic being directed by way of Queensferry Street. Here the sign 'Trams only' is protecting what was perhaps the UK's shortest 'reserved track tramway'. Behind, car 317 is from a batch of twenty supplied by the English Electric Company in 1924.

46. Bob Parr must have taken his life in his hands to stand in the roadway to take this evocative shot, which can be timed, precisely, at 4.04 pm on 1 August 1952. Car 337 was built in 1925 and was scrapped in April 1953 after withdrawal of routes 2 and 3. Note that it carries two front slip boards.

47. George Street in August is now never as quiet as this; but on the 8th of that month in 1952 car 337 (again) has little traffic to contend with. The statue of William Pitt can – on not infrequent occasions – gaze imperturbably down on the latest manifestation of traffic management in Scotland's capital – gridlock.

48. December 14 1952, the date of this photograph, was the last day of use of George Street by trams. It was as popular then for parking as it is now! On the corner of Frederick Street, the site of the Sun Alliance insurance development lay undeveloped for many years, the building not being completed until 1955. Car 338 heading for Stenhouse.

WAVERLEY&COMELY BANK

24

49. Only one service, 24, used the tracks from Frederick Street to Comely Bank, hence it was a logical first abandonment, its last car running on 31 May 1952. In the city centre cars ran in via George Street and South St. Andrew Street then back by Princes Street and Frederick Street. In 1951 the manual points in Princes Street were upgraded; henceforth the driver pushed a switch on the pole to change them as seen in this view. They then returned automatically to their former position after the car had passed.

50. Car 89 reaches the high point of its journey – the Frederick Street and George Street crossing, on the last day of operation. Some original New Town architecture is clearly visible in the houses (which mostly became shops or offices) behind. Purists objected to the George Street statues (George IV, Pitt, and Chalmers, from east to west) being enclosed in the tram overhead and were pleased to see it removed. The tram has a panel prepared for an advert, but it is yet to be applied.

51. Queen Street Gardens south of Howe Street indicating the gradient that made this street too steep for horse trams, thus necessitating the second of Edinburgh's cable car routes. Car 275 climbs the hill above Heriot Row while a cyclist, wisely, pushes his bike up the hill. The car is one of the few without the lower deck rubbing strip.

52. Car 32 climbs through the leafy gardens of Royal Circus on its ascent from Stockbridge. Residents of these elegant crescents perhaps considered the first cable cars to be an intrusion into the calm gentility of the area, but there was no argument with regard to their utility. The street today still has its setts with the path of the former tramway clearly defined. The buildings in the distance form the east side of Howe Street.

53. Again – to judge by the lack of traffic – a Sunday scene, but even then the 24 frequency was a car every 6 minutes (but the first car did not run until just before 10.00 am). The tram is leaving Kerr Street to cross the Water of Leith bridge. The tenements on the right were demolished in 1967, the site now landscaped. Hamilton Place, off to the left, was used by cable trams to gain access to their depot in Henderson Row.

54. Car 275 approaches Comely Bank terminus, in August 1950, the destination screen already turned to show 'Waverley'. Moir & Baxter's garage behind the tram has now been demolished and replaced by new brick built housing. Note the bicycling policeman – a sight recently returned to the city streets – but with a 21st century mount.

55. Last day of service 24, 31st May 1952 was the first time since abandonment of the Port Seton line in 1928 that the citizens of Edinburgh had lost any part of their tram system. Note the bus stop on the right 'Service 9 only'. When the last day arrived the paint squad came to paint bus orange over the red stripes on poles denoting tram stops. Unfortunately these had only been freshly painted red the previous day – the paint was not even dry!

56. Car 31 at the very end of the line, with Craigleith Road stretching westwards. There had been plans many years before for an electric tramway extending from the West End (and Comely Bank) to beyond South Queensferry, but these were given up after the First World War. Service 24 was much used by staff and visitors to the nearby Royal Victoria and Western General hospitals.

57. On the final day the conductor of car 235 swings the trolley pole round while enjoying a fly puff. The bus is creeping into the scene; on route 9 is 222 (HSG172), an AEC Regent III with Brockhouse bodywork, then just two years old. A design which, although twenty years younger that that of the tram, seems to complement the tram rather than conflict with it.

58. The second phase of tram abandonment featured routes using Dalry Road ie services 2, 3 and 4. In July 1952 car 320 heads west to Stenhouse with passengers both boarding and leaving the car on Gorgie Road at the top of Westfield Road. The well-proportioned sandstone block on the left was built in 1925.

59. Car 337 displays 'Saughton Rose Garden' boards on its inward journey to the City centre and on to Granton. Pausing to uplift passengers at Chesser Avenue, with behind the old leather works and tanneries which used the nearby Water of Leith. These old buildings have been replaced by office developments, Riverside House and Chesser House.

60. At the Stenhouse Road terminus with its 1928-29 council housing development which guaranteed good passenger figures (but not enough to secure its existence). Powers were granted in 1936 to extend the line to the city boundary at Sighthill, which with the considerable volume of council house construction underway would have been of great benefit. Overhead poles were installed but the extension was postponed by the outbreak of World War Two and never completed.

61. The other service to reach Stenhouse was the 3, from Newington station. Here car 332, in September 1952, just six months before closure, is busily loading from the island opposite the West End clock. Following outcry when the clock was removed a timepiece of remarkable kitsch with revolving model pipers was added to the corner of the House of Fraser store.

62. The Balgreen Road/Hutchison Crossway stop – alight here for the renowned Saughton Rose Garden – still to this day an oasis of beauty and tranquillity. In past days the perfume from the roses 'combated' the pungent local brewery aromas. Car 165 advertises BEA '...to London for the Continent...'. Following is Daimler CVG6, FSC176 on route 5 to Sighthill.

63. Car 302 waiting its turn to reverse at Stenhouse Road terminus on a bleak winter day – to judge by the leafless trees and well wrapped up pedestrians. Today's traffic has altered radically what was then a relatively quiet scene, albeit the main road from Edinburgh to West Calder and Kilmarnock. This route was much used by visitors to inmates of (then) His Majesty's prison, just to the right.

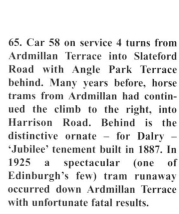

64. Last of the routes serving Dalry Road to be abandoned was service 4, from Slateford to Piershill or Kings Road. Here car 177 heads traffic out of town at the entrance to Dalry cemetery – passing Coffin Lane off to the right. Note the period Ovaltine and Players adverts. The over-bridge which then carried the LMS Leith branch railway now serves the motor age, as part of the Western Approach relief road, opened in December 1974.

65. Car 58 on service 4 turns from Ardmillan Terrace into Slateford Road with Angle Park Terrace behind. Many years before, horse trams from Ardmillan had continued the climb to the right, into Harrison Road. Behind is the distinctive ornate – for Dalry – 'Jubilee' tenement built in 1887. In 1925 a spectacular (one of Edinburgh's few) tram runaway occurred down Ardmillan Terrace with unfortunate fatal results.

66. Seen from Slateford Station at the terminus of service 4 is car 269, the highest numbered of its type. This was also the terminus of Edinburgh's first electric line, built in 1910. It ran through open fields, council house building in the vicinity not starting until 1927. Tram extension westwards was frustrated by low railway and canal bridges, but a northwards extension along Chesser Avenue was authorised as early as 1908.

67. The Dalry Road and Corstorphine services diverged at Haymarket, where 310 collects passengers heading west. Behind is the Heart of Midlothian war memorial clock, which was moved to its present position in 1972 to assist traffic flow. Not much traffic however in this July 1954 scene. Until two years earlier services 25 and 26 ran to Drum Brae South but that terminus was considered a traffic hazard.

68. It was quite unusual for 'wooden standard' type cars to be used on service 12. This view was taken on 10 July 1954, a week before abandonment of the Corstorphine trams and bus stop signs are already in place at Roseburn Bridge. (The new bridge was built in 1841 and widened in the 1930s – the old bridge now carries no traffic and is just a few yards downstream.) Unusual combination following with car 25 on service 25!

CORSTORPHINE. FOOT OF LEITH WALK.
AND KING'S ROAD

69. Car 137 on the lengthy service 1 (eight miles) from Corstorphine to Liberton seen at 'Western Corner' on 24 May 1953. Here Ellersley Road and Saughtonhall Drive meet Corstorphine Road. Formerly the city boundary before the extensions of the 1920 Act, this was the terminus for cable cars until extended, on electrification, in June 1923 to Templeland Road.

70. Three specials at the Zoo Park entrance on 18 April 1954. Ex Manchester 411 is on a special LRTL tour which took it on many tracks where its type had never previously ventured (including Corstorphine). It is flanked by two of the many extra cars which were run most weekends and holidays, from Waverley to the Zoo only.

26

PIERSHILL & DRUM BRAE SOUTH

71. St. John's Road, Corstorphine on 24 May 1953, a view which shows clearly the extent of the road widening which was undertaken thirty years earlier when the tramways were laid. (Even today this is still a 'pinch' point on the A8 trunk road.) This, however, looks like a Sunday morning view with but a solitary motor vehicle parked at the tram stop. ('Cars from town stop here' – just in case one's sense of direction was completely lacking.)

CORSTORPHINE & KING'S ROAD

72. St John's Road at the foot of Clermiston Road with tram 285 heading west on service 25 to Corstorphine. In addition to its 'Zoo Park' board it boasts also 'To and From the Coronation Ice Carnival at Murrayfield Ice Rink'. Note also the elderly Rolls Royce at Station Road and the bicycle on the front platform of the tram.

73. May 1951 scene at the Corstorphine Glasgow Road terminus. Trams were extended here in February 1937, in advance of the spec housing which was delayed by World War Two. To the east of the old Maybury Garage can be seen open fields stretching north into the distance – covered in the 1950's by the North Gyle bungalows. At this time the NCB laboratories were still to be built.

74. The open space seen here at the Corstorphine Maybury terminus forms a remarkable contrast with today's major road junction with its forest of traffic lights and road direction signs. In the distance, the listed Art Deco factory built for Thompson & Norris Ltd (corrugated paper and box makers) in 1934 which is now operated by a Swedish organisation, SCA.

75. Variously known as 'The Register', The Post Office', 'GPO' or the 'East End', the junction at the foot of North Bridge was a focal point of Edinburgh's tram system with many services passing to Princes Street and many others using the Bridges. Control was by a pointsman whose box is just seen behind the tramcar.

76. The bulk of the late Victorian North British Hotel building looms over the corner of North Bridge and Princes Street. Here car 351 en route to Granton collects its passengers from the loading island at the Crawford's branch fifty years ago. Note the red on yellow side board – an example of which is preserved at the National Tramway Museum at Crich in Derbyshire.

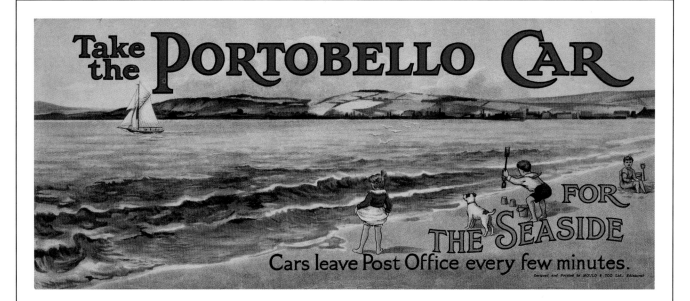

77. A very intensive service was given on services 20 and 21 (with part-day 22 until 1946) from here at Waterloo Place to Joppa, Musselburgh and Levenhall. The 20 ran at least every 2½ minutes, with the other services in addition. At weekends, holidays etc, there were also many 'extras' to Portobello. It was most unusual to see the terminus without at least one car waiting to come forward as soon as the previous one was filled. Car 405 was purchased from Manchester Corporation in 1948, and looked much better after reconstruction at Shrubhill than it had on arrival.

78. King's Road, Portobello, in 1951 with car 97 on service 20 to Joppa. Behind is the remarkable tenemental terrace (Kings Road) slipping down the cul-de-sac to the Promenade. The Firth of Forth can be seen in the distance. Note the red painted stripe on the pole to indicate the tram stop (which to the end retained a unique '1d Fare Stage' sign).

79. The same locus, but with, in the foreground car 173 on service 15. It is about to turn right into Portobello High Street, reverse there to return to Fairmilehead. The conductor has already set the destination screen. Behind, a car on service 12 crosses to begin its unimpeded race along Seafield Road en route to Leith and then to Corstorphine.

80. At King's Road Portobello is ex Manchester 'Pilcher' car 411; so called after its designer R. Stewart Pilcher, the former Edinburgh manager who masterminded the cable/electric transformation. Behind rises the red brick bulk of Portobello power station built in 1921 to supply power for the tramway electrification. Warmed 'cooling water' was used in the adjacent open-air swimming pool of fond memory. The Power Station was demolished in 1979, the site now occupied by housing.

81. Having just reversed, car 195 pauses at the King's Road loading island before setting off on its lengthy trip across the city to Braids (for which the fare until December 1951 was only 3d). Behind the telephone box is the red brick Ramsay Technical Institute – said to have been built as a chocolate factory. Under the road was a railway tunnel for loaded coal wagons for the power station.

POST OFFICE - PORTOBELLO
MUSSELBURGH - LEVENHALL

82. Joppa, terminus of route 20 from the GPO, was at the eastern end of Portobello Promenade. Formerly the limit of cable car operation, it was the point where passengers had to change to the green cars of the Musselburgh District Tramways which ran trams as far as Port Seton until February 1928. The tracks were joined in 1923 and for five further years through cars were operated by both undertakings. Two crossovers were provided to cope with busy periods, when cars on route 12 also ran through to Joppa.

CORSTORPHINE. FOOT OF LEITH WALK
KINGS ROAD AND JOPPA.

83. Edinburgh trams ran for over two miles along the A1 through Musselburgh. Here, at Musselburgh Race Course, car 197 has the thoroughfare virtually to itself. The last section was of single track with loops, which required the cautionary signs (left) erected at the time of wartime blackout restrictions.

84. Service 21 was given a certain distinction in its latter years by the use of these 'Pilcher' ex-Manchester cars. (Only very occasionally were they used on the short working 20 to Joppa.) Car 406 (former Manchester 217) pauses at the end of Linkfield Road while it waits for the Levenhall terminus round the corner to be vacated by the preceding car. The motor car heading up the A1 towards Tranent is not taking as much risk as may be thought, as the motorist will be aware that the tram is not likely to move off suddenly.

85. Nearing Levenhall car 120 – a Portobello depot stalwart – waits outside Forman's Inn until the lengthy single track leading to the terminus is cleared. At this point the main A1 leads off to Tranent, the subject of unfulfilled tramway proposals before the First World War. Now trading as Mrs Forman's, the Inn has had its appearance changed with an overall coat of white paint, but still is as popular. The main road no longer passes quite so close to the front door of the hostelry.

86. Right at the end of the line, car 167 and another wait to return to the city – a 35 minute, 7½ mile trip for which the fare was raised from 3d to 5d (2p) in December 1951. Behind the photographer, the former Musselburgh Company tramway had continued further four miles along the coastal road (B1348) to Prestonpans and Port Seton.

87. The heyday of Edinburgh's trams in the immediate post-war period. Several people wait at the stop for the next 23 or 27 car to Lauriston and Tollcross. Note the diligently observed 'Q this side/Q other side' instructions posted on the tram stop pole.

88. Edinburgh trams seemed to suit Edinburgh architecture. All is changed from this scene – the trams have gone, as have the distinctive facades – replaced by 'Panel' abominations when the 1958 dictat was to provide a pedestrian walkway at first floor level. This came to naught, leaving several meaningless 'balconies' on bland 1950's and 60's structures. To the left the New Club facade dating from 1834; closer to the camera the 1855 Life Association Ltd building, which for many years boasted two enormous cast iron street lights of singular Victorian ungainliness.

89. Car 235 heading for Morningside Station passes the entrance to Edinburgh Royal Infirmary in Lauriston Place. A tram was run – at visiting hours only – from Hanover Street to this crossover. Note the number 15 Juniper Green bus also in shot, and behind it the bulk of the University Medical School in Teviot Place.

90. Car 169 in Lauriston Place at the top of Lady Lawson Street. Behind the sub-post office rises the hose tower of the red sandstone Central Fire Station, practically the only element of the scene which has not vanished. The block on the left was replaced by the truly hideous six storey Lauriston House, built in 1960 and inhabited largely by the NCB. Now standing empty, it currently looks ripe for demolition. The right hand terrace has also gone, overtaken by the Hunter Building of Edinburgh College of Art.

91. Points policeman – complete with white visibility 'cuffs' – directing traffic at the busy intersection of Lauriston Place and Brougham Street, Tollcross. The 'Tollcross' pub with its Ekcovision advert was flattened and a Goldberg store erected – only for the area to then stagnate, even Goldberg's has since been demolished. On the right the former tenement block with the fondly remembered 'Elizabeth' restaurant (a name which sums up the patriotic feelings of the time, only a few years after the Coronation) has been demolished and replaced by a bland brick block. Long shadows in this summer 1956 scene.

92. Car 180 poses outside Tollcross depot. This imposing red sandstone building was built as one of the major power stations for the cable trams. Dating from 1899 it was converted to electric car use, then for use by buses. It ceased to be used for buses in 1969 and was demolished shortly thereafter. Note the stone carved lettering above the window arch.

93. A fine interior view of Tollcross Depot, which was in use until the last day of tram operation. Its original cable car layout made it a quite difficult conversion, with two distinct areas, the tracks at right angles in each part. This view is of the former engine house, with much greater headroom than required for the electric trams. The corbels carried a massive overhead crane, necessary during cable days but remaining in place, unused, long after these days were over.

94. The Tollcross of the 1950s has changed considerably since these record photos were exposed. Tramcar 15 has to be compared with the Leyland PD2 behind which was the standard vehicle purchased for most of the tram replacement programme... an improvement?

95. The passing scene at Tollcross was always full of fascination – the procession of trams – so much similarity but so much variety. The only building remaining is the tenement on the right at the start of Home Street. Passing in front of Grant's grocers, is a lorry load of beer from Murray's Brewery at Craigmillar (see the side adverts on pages 91 and 92).

96. Car 180 passing Tollcross on the same day, heading to Braids on service 28. The Shrubhill built tram drew wonderment when it was first run on the streets of the capital – but who in 1956 gave it a second glance? Perhaps somebody in authority thought it deserved a better fate that its compatriots – but this was not to be and it suffered the ignominy of a one-way trip to Connell's 'tramatorium' in Coatbridge on 7 January 1957 – one of the last to go from Shrubhill.

97. Car 265, similar, but far from identical to 180 above, also photographed at Tollcross. The track connection which led round by Thornybauk to West Tollcross gave an alternative access to the depot and was mostly used by cars entering service. This had formed the access to the depot in its cable car days.

98. Route 27 cars from Granton Road Station originally terminated here at 'Firrhill', the junction of Colinton Road with Colinton Mains Drive where car 47 is seen. There had at one time been a proposal for a tram-road from here to Braids terminus but like many such proposals it came to nothing.

99. The Colinton extension, opened in March 1926, ran through (then) quiet roads past Redford Barracks (on the right) and the grounds of Merchiston Castle School on the left. The last section of the route consisted of – unusually for Edinburgh – single track and passing loops. No other road traffic disturbs this (Sunday?) scene of car 40 heading for the terminus.

100. Streamline car 27 on service 10 drops off passengers at Redford Road as it nears the terminus. The first proposal for a tramway to Colinton (from Craiglockhart with a link to Slateford also) envisaged a private right of way on this wide roadside verge. Use of the proposed tramway right of way was made by the contractor Colin McAndrew for a temporary railway to supply building materials when Redford Barracks was under construction.

101. The other service to reach Colinton was the 9 from Granton. Here car 193 of 1922 vintage – one of the earliest standard cars built for electrification – waits to gain access to the terminal single track stub to reverse for its return journey. Approaching in the distance a green SMT double deck bus heading for Balerno.

This 1920's poster is a reminder of the days when to reach Colinton village it was necessary to change to a bus at the Craiglockart tram terminus.

102. Hurst Nelson built car 239 waits to reverse at Colinton terminus before returning to Granton on service 10. Note the yellow board 'Via Leith Walk'. This car carried an unusual word transposition advertisement 'Have a ticket that's the Capstan'.

103. The line through the Meadows was attractive in all seasons. From Tollcross as far as Marchmont Road service 6 shared the tracks with service 19 to Craigentinny Avenue, and until March 1950 also with service 18 to Liberton Dams. The 6 ran a basic five-minute frequency in both directions with eight cars on the inner and eight on the outer to provide this density. Service 6 was withdrawn on 26 May 1956. Car 204 was allocated to Tollcross depot for its entire working life but was withdrawn a month prior to final abandonment.

104. The unique 180 seen again, this time at the Bruntsfield short working terminus in Merchiston Place which took part route cars off the main line to Churchhill. The stub was built in 1926 as a terminus for service 23, but after this was extended to Morningside Station in 1929 the line had no regular use. Photographed on an enthusiasts' special working.

105. 'Holy Corner' with car 180 heading into town and a taxi turning into Colinton Road. Actually a crossroads rather than a 'corner', it got its name from its four churches – one to each corner. Two of these can be seen here as 'Red Biddy' makes its way northwards. Behind, the Congregational Church on the corner of Chamberlain Road is now Morningside United Church, while to the right is North Morningside – now the Eric Liddell Centre. The tenements form the south end of Bruntsfield Place.

106. Time to talk, then – not a good idea today at this busy junction. Car 221 operating on service 23 is just about to turn right into its terminus at Belhaven Terrace, Morningside Station which it shared with service 5. The station building on the Suburban railway can be seen on the left. It retained its passenger train service until 1962, six years after the trams had gone. A Sunday scene to judge by the drawn blinds on R S McColl's shop. The fabric of the scene has changed little over the years; although McColl has gone the newsagent facility remains in different hands.

107. Deserted streets (another Sunday?) as car 120 returns to town down Comiston Road, just where the road narrows to cross the Braid Burn. The road widening undertaken in the 1930s came to an end here. Note the 'Request' stop which has had the Bus Stop sign recently added.

108. Car 137 about to reverse at the 'Braids' crossover on Sunday 12 August 1956. Always known thus, the terminus was quite a step from Braid Hills, but was the closest that most people could get by tram to one of Edinburgh's popular 'lungs', purchased by the City in 1890.

109. Classic 1956 pose at Fairmilehead terminus – classic tram – classic style pink dress of the posing lady passenger. Car 214 is on service 11 to Stanley Road. This terminus was much used by visitors to the Princess Margaret Rose Hospital in Frogston Road. Service 11 operated on a 10-minute frequency from before 7 am to midnight.

110. On 15 July 1955 buses had already made their appearance at Fairmilehead. Car 202, also on service 11, has as company a Leyland PD2 operating tram replacement service 15 which had been changed over during the previous September. Authority was obtained in 1934 to extend this route to Hillend Park, hence the terminus was built as double track.

111. Another classic scene; car 55 at Liberton terminus in 1951, with in the distance the 'Lion's Haunch' of Arthur's Seat – Edinburgh's own volcano. The double track terminal layout again indicated the intention to extend south – authority had been granted before the Second World War for a ¾-mile length to Kaimes, the junction of Captain's Road. On the right the railings of Dr Guthrie's School.

112. Car 231 on service 7 at Liberton terminus, 15 July 1955. The car became notable for its unique 'Zoo' adverts. On this side four penguins chased a pelican exhorting 'You too can dine at the Zoo' while the other side had another piece of the Shrubhill sign writer's artistry – four elephants carrying a banner emblazoned 'Don't forget to visit – the Zoo'.

113. Newington Station, at the start of Craigmillar Park was terminus for services 3, 8 and 17 (also sometime 18). Car 138 having crossed over to return to town waits by the 'Cars To Town' sign amongst the flurries of winter snow of February 1955.

114. Car 252 on service 17 also at Newington Station. The 8 and 17 services shared this terminus but while the former ran via Broughton Street and Goldenacre to Granton, the latter ran via Foot of Leith Walk, Bernard Street and Newhaven. A better day, with the conductress's summer white top cap in evidence.

115. Eastern terminus of service 19 was 'on the waterfront' at Craigentinny Avenue North. Car 264 is waiting to cross to the inbound track for its run up the Bridges and along Melville Drive to Tollcross. This stop was much used by staff and visitors to the Eastern General Hospital – off to the right. The seaward side here is much altered with acres of land reclaimed from the foreshore – for Edinburgh's new sewage disposal works.

116. Car 216 also at Craigentinny Avenue North, reversing for its trip to Tollcross. Service 19, in this form, dated from October 1935 only. A previous 19 service had operated Newington Station to Morningside Station via Princes Street until July 1929. Placed in service in July 1939, car 216 always operated from Leith Depot until the closure of the system.

117. Facing Union Place is Greenside Place, best known perhaps as the home of Edinburgh's largest cinema, the Playhouse. With over 3000 seats it was designed to also serve as a theatre. To the right is Lady Glenorchy's Low Calton Church. Following disuse as a place of worship it stood derelict for many years, then the Church was demolished, with the facade only retained, supported by steel props. Happily, at last, the site is now being developed.

118. Union Place (seen here) and Greenside Place (behind the photographer), formed the top end of Leith Walk. All this block of Union Place and most of Greenside Place were demolished by 1973, falling victim in the preparations for Edinburgh's never realised Inner Ring Road. Only now is life returning to some of these blighted areas. The Deep Sea restaurant was a (in)famous fish and chip emporium. Note the centre poles with Leith Corporation arms on their bases. They were relocated from Great Junction Street after the 1920 amalgamation but retained these obvious traces of their previous owners.

LEITH DOCKS

119. Bernard Street swing bridge was always a source of interest. Originally with 'catch' points to prevent any stray tramcar descending into the depths of the Water of Leith, these were removed latterly. However power was cut off from the overhead for some yards back from the 'brink'. Behind, the 'Shore' has been rejuvenated with new flats and many popular eating-houses, but in the 1950s this remained part of a busy working port.

120. Views of the bridge open for traffic on the Water of Leith are few and far between. The movable roadway section, complete with tram overhead, can be seen when it was opened to allow the motor cruiser 'Mona' through. Note the Tramways Dept tower wagon on standby in the background and the lads lying on the cabin roof!

121. More typical scene with the bridge firmly in the road position. Behind is the early 19th century Leith Custom House in Commercial Street. The old opening bridge has been replaced by a fixed concrete construction, curtailing greatly the upstream use which is also now no longer tidal.

122. Car 23 on a short working prepares to reverse in Commercial Street to return to the Post Office. Here at Leith North Station there was a double track railway across the tramway, entering the docks to the right. These William Muir Bond 9 or 'Highland Queen' bonded warehouses have entered a new lease of life with the regeneration of the area and have been converted to up-market flats.

123. The level crossing and dock gates in Commercial Street (for some years 'Dock Gates' was shown as a destination, while there were many Dock Gates, this is what was meant!). Behind the tram are the buildings of what was then Leith Nautical College, now (with a 1981 extension to the east) functioning as the corporate headquarters of the Gregor Group.

124. Empty loading island at the junction of Commercial Street and North Junction Street (off to the right). In tram terminology this locus was 'Caledonian Station Leith'. The blank wall of the Station is visible to the left – complete with famous Guinness poster. Car 55 on service 16 to Granton, an arrangement which existed only from 16 June until 11 September 1956.

125. Newhaven Pier Place with tramway to the left, one-way (now cul-de-sac) Main Street to the right. Further to the right, the tram track connection into Craighall Road. This link had not been used by any regular service for many years. The semi circular end of former 'Marine Hotel' still dominates the scene, but now roughcast and turned into flats. In the right background another tram turns into Newhaven's Fish Market Square.

126. Trinity Bridge with its notorious single line tramway Z-bend snaking below the railway bridge. Car 37 heading for Braids during the last summer of service 16, and, indeed, all tramway operation. Even with the bridge and its approach embankments now removed, for some unfathomable reason the bend and traffic light control still remains as a traffic obstruction fifty years later.

127. Despite signals the occasional unplanned event did take place here! A meeting of crews is examining the points while the two cars have a confrontation. A bystander on the right finds the view over the Forth of much more absorbing interest! The further car is 239. Note the air-raid siren still fixed to the overhead pole behind the tram (it is not mounted on the tram roof). Car 201 appears to have failed just beyond the points which are defeating the crew's attempts to shift them to get the car back out of the way.

128. At the foot of Craighall Road car 160 waits its starting time. With virtually no traffic potential this street saw little use after 1920, until services 7, 11 and 28 were extended down from Stanley Road in October 1949. This was probably done solely to ease congestion in that narrow street.

129. The previous terminus was located here at the west end of Stanley Road. Here car 248 is heading for Braids on service 28 during the last months of tram operation. Note the 'skate' on the overhead, used in conjunction with lights to control the single track curve into Craighall Road; a similar arrangement was provided at the east end of Stanley Road where there was another single track right angled bend into Newhaven Road.

130. The west end of Lower Granton Road, stop-over timing point for 13 (outer) and 14 (inner) Granton/Churchhill services. Always a busy location, with three crossovers and cars either passing through (services 13&14) or reversing (services 2, 8, 9, 16 & 17). Here is tram 260 in company with former NBR locomotive 64479.

131. Partner of 260 was 265 – a pair of steel bodied cars built by Metro-Cammel in 1933 in similar style to Edinburgh's own 180. In Granton Square, 8 August 1955, with to the right the building used by the RNVR as HMS Claverhouse which was built many years before as the Granton Inn.

132. Car 239 was yet another manifestation of the seemingly infinitely varying appearance of the Edinburgh tram before it finalised in the 1934 design typified by 157 (to the right) on service 9 to Colinton via Broughton Street. 239 (built by Hurst Nelson) is on service 10 to Colinton and exhibits its yellow 'via Leith Walk' front board.

133. Streamlined car 24 about to reverse on the central Granton crossover to commence its journey to Colinton. Granton Harbour coal yards are to the right with, behind the tram, the central pier of the Duke of Buccleuch's 1835 harbour development. From here both coal and ice were loaded into the large fleet of steam trawlers which used Granton as their base.

134. Car 23 in May 1951 climbs the long steady grade up Granton Road from the terminus at the foot of the hill. Superb panoramic views are to be found and a trip round the Granton Circle was a pleasurable way of spending a Sunday afternoon – all for 3d! The open area on the left today is filled by the upper storeys of the former Ferranti offices in Lower Granton Road, which although not built when this photograph was recorded, have now been standing empty for many years.

135. Granton Road was virtually open countryside when Leith Corporation built this tramway in 1909. It was not until construction of the East Pilton, Wardie, Boswall and Grierson council schemes in the 1930's that traffic levels increased. Car 196 heading north at Granton Road Station.

136. Evocative night shot of car 37 crossing Princes Street from Hanover Street to the Mound on route to Morningside Station. The specifically 'Edinburgh' route colours show well how the scheme benefited the waiting passenger. Routes could be distinguished for a considerable distance and the various colour permutations were even used as a memory test for some City Brownie packs!

137. Older cars carried this sign at the top of the platform handrail – but who paid any heed? One of the great benefits of the tram was the ability to get off and on while the car was travelling – but the critical element was always to face forwards – the direction of travel – before leaping off!

TRAM
WEEK

LAST
TRAM
WEEK

LAST
TRAM
WEEK

LAST
TRAM
WEEK

LAST
TRAM
WEEK

LAST
TRAM
WEEK

LAST
TRAM
WEEK

LAST
TRAM
WEEK

138. No colour shots (other than some cine film excerpts) have come forward of decorated tram 172 as it toured the remaining fragments of the tram system during the final week in November 1956. Seen coming down Home Street with a tower wagon in close attendance. Perhaps the poor weather of that week discouraged colour photography. Veteran driver Bill Moffat drove it during that final week.

139. The design of Edinburgh's ultimate decorated tram was entrusted to the College of Art, whose Mr. S. Barry produced the restrained, 'ghostly' but discrete design utilising five hundred 12 watt bulbs. Seen in Lauriston Place leaving Tollcross.

"Ma auld feyther aye said this day would come . . . an' tae think Ah never believed him!"

140. From the same vantage point as the scene on page 74, this final night scene shows just some of the enormous crowds that turned out – not to celebrate, but to mourn the end of an epoch. The restored horse bus precedes 172 – still without passengers – it travelled its complete last week without taking a single fare. The crowds filling Hanover Street will not see the like again.

'TIM' tickets were introduced to the trams in 1933 – this is one of the first. Bus tickets were printed in green.

This ticket was issued for one of the trams of the final procession.

CITY AND ROYAL BURGH OF EDINBURGH
TRANSPORT DEPARTMENT

OPERATION OF LAST TRAM,
Friday, 16th November 1956.

This card is available on Reserved Car

No.......1.......from Braids at....7:20....p.m.

61—11/56

W. M. LITTLE,
Transport Manager.

141. What a waste – Connell's scrap yard in Lock Street Coatbridge, where most of the redundant trams were reduced to their basic elements by burning.

142. Lifting of remaining tracks was undertaken in most principal streets with considerable haste. The last major piece of track remained in Lauriston Place until the end of 1959. A short length of cable track has been reinstated in Waterloo Place where it serves as Edinburgh's only visible reminder of tramway days.

143. Edinburgh standard 35 was saved from scrap. It was the third choice for preservation. The first choice had been 225 – the last car built at Shrubhill – but it was badly damaged in a smash just two months before final closure; second choice 172 had just been repainted as the decorated 'last tram'. 35 was the 'star' (but static) exhibit in the Transport Department museum from 1961 to 1979. In late 1983 it was taken to Blackpool for that system's centenary the next year. Also there was 1297, the pride of the Glasgow tram system. Needless to say a race along the Prom was arranged which took place on 12 April 1984. Driver Michael Pass of the winning Edinburgh tram was presented with a haggis as his reward.

144. Since 1988 preserved Edinburgh tramcar 35 has been kept at the National Tramway Museum at Crich near Matlock in Derbyshire. This view in the summer of 2000 shows it to be in good external condition, but unfortunately it is not considered as fit for operation, with electrical wiring being less than satisfactory. There are, however, many other operational trams to choose from – so don't be put off visiting the Museum just because 35 is not at present in use.

145. Former (electrified) cable car 226 was acquired in 1938 to fulfil a second life as a holiday home at Hume Castle in the Borders. Cared for by three generations of the Goodfellow family, they eventually parted with it in order that it might be restored to its former state. In this springtime view it forms an oasis of tranquillity in its retirement. The cost of acquisition and transport was met by Lothian Region Transport and the National Museums of Scotland.

146. In December 1987 the tram made its way back to the City to start the long reconstruction process. Through the good will of Lothian Region Transport, and their successors, Lothian Buses plc, space has been made available and the long and costly process of restoration has commenced. It is seen nearing the end of its journey home.

THE CARS

To the uninitiated, in their twilight years, all Edinburgh trams appeared remarkably alike, the only exception in the last few months of operation being car 180.

The 1934 'standard' car was the final stage in what had been a period of considerable experimentation and development in the early 1930's. Because of the continued use of the cable tram system (until it was well past its sell-by date), when electrification of the City tramways took place in 1922-23, a fleet of trams was created of two distinct types; new built and reconstructed former cable cars. The specification for each type was remarkably alike and, while the cars employed the latest motors, controllers and wheel designs, these, plus design of bodywork had changed little throughout the previous twenty years. The resulting 'standard' car had a recognisable style which compared favourably with the design used in Glasgow and which had been developed there more or less continuously during twenty-five years of electric tram operation.

Hence Edinburgh had (in its new built cars) a design featuring open balcony top deck construction, enclosed driver platform and a lower saloon seating 22 on wooden longitudinal seats plus further 36 seats on the upper deck. Motors were two of 40hp, in Peckham 8ft 6in. wheelbase trucks with (usually) 27-inch diameter wheels. The evolved Glasgow 'Standard' of this era is difficult (perhaps only for an Edinburgh person) to classify precisely, but the S.J.T. Robertson defined "Phase 3 Standard Tram" would perhaps be closest for comparison purposes – with a tram of similar specification for bodywork, but seating 24 in the saloon, and 38 on the upper deck. Motors were mostly of 45hp and trucks of the 21E style (which itself dated back over twenty-five years) of 7ft 0in. wheelbase.

Within two years of the end of cable operation just over two hundred former cable cars were converted at Shrubhill works, and further ninety-two trams were purchased from outside contractors. Thereafter Shrubhill began to construct new electric cars to similar design but gradually introducing change. The apparently random numbering of Edinburgh's tram fleet was probably an accounting foible, where replacement cars took the number of the car replaced and were paid for from the Revenue Account, while cars added to stock were numbered separately at the end of the numerical sequence, and were purchased from Capital funds.

Towards the end of 1931 the Town Council authorised £4000 be spent on a new modern tramcar. Their forward looking policy (at a time when many tramway undertakings were being closed) confirmed that the Council was fully aware of the benefits derived from their tramway system, and having just committed large sums to the cable conversion, were continuing their positive stance. The car, numbered 180, appeared from Shrubhill at the end of March 1932 – the body cost only £2020.13s – and it was given a second-hand truck, although new controllers were fitted. Not only was a 12% overall weight reduction achieved through considerable use of aluminium alloys, but seating was increased to 64 or by nearly 10%. Car 180 was the precursor of a number of differing cars from outside contractors. Thereafter Shrubhill produced yet another one-off design, car 261.

From all these the manager and his chief draughtsman, Mr Harold Mittell developed the design of car 69 which appeared before the end of 1934, forming the basis for a style of tram which continued to be constructed at Shrubhill until 1950. A total of 84 were built, all similar but with variation in ventilation top deck window style etc. Even more use was made of aluminium in this design, with several special alloy castings incorporated. Side panels were of 'Armourply' laminated timber/aluminium sheets. All took numbers of earlier cars. In the last months approaching abandonment some of the earliest examples were scrapped before the final day.

To fill a short term need eleven cars were obtained from Manchester Corporation in 1947-9 and given numbers 401-411. It is understood that only ten were initially bargained for, but one that had been intended for Aberdeen and was rejected by them as being in too poor condition, eventually became Edinburgh's eleventh car.

By mid 1956 therefore, with the exception of 180, only the 1934 style standard tram was in evidence. A proposal to purchase some of these by Dundee Corporation was not followed through and all, with the notable exception of number 35, were scrapped. This survivor can currently be seen at the National Tramway Museum at Crich in Derbyshire.

For complete details of the Edinburgh tram fleet in all its complexity, the interested reader is referred to 'Edinburgh's Transport – The Corporation Years' by D.L.G. Hunter, also published by, and available from Adam Gordon: see details at the end of this volume.

CONDUCTORS ARE INSTRUCTED NOT TO ALLOW CHILDREN TO STAND ON CAR SEATS.

147. The second lowest numbered car in revenue stock was one of twenty contracted for in 1935 from three external suppliers, of a similar design to three supplied the previous year. Number 12 went into service in September, working from Leith Depot for all of its days. It was withdrawn from service in mid June 1956. 'Maitland Radio' was only advertised on a few vehicles, a relatively small business based at Gayfield Place.

148. Car 18 was from the batch of eight (11-18) built by Hurst Nelson & Co of Motherwell. It entered service in November 1935 and ran as a Leith Depot car until scrapped, also in June 1956. McVitie & Price was another of Edinburgh's renowned bakers. Their name is still to the fore, although the business is now part of United Biscuits.

149. Streamlined car 27 was from a batch of six built by Metropolitan-Cammel Ltd of Birmingham. They had detail differences from those of other builders, the most noticeable being the corner mounted service number screen. All were initially allocated to Portobello depot on delivery in September 1935. Early during the war years the Portobello six were taken over by Leith Depot where they completed their years of use. 27 was scrapped in April 1956. Note the conductor turning the trolley and the pennants flying from the trolley rope.

150. Number 29 of the same batch in Princes St, is followed by 168 which was, belied by its appearance, only five years older. When these streamlined cars appeared initially in service, the upper deck livery was reversed, with the lower portion white and the upper, including the sweep down to the destination box, in madder. 29 ran from September 1935 to April 1956, its use and allocation as car 27 above.

151. Car 37 at Granton on service 14. It is of the 'post war' standard style and had a short life, from February 1949 until the end of operation in November 1956. It lay in Shrubhill for a month being removed for scrap on Boxing Day. (In those far-off days when both Christmas and Boxing Days were normal working days in Scotland!)

152. Car 40 in Princes Street on a Sunday morning. Placed in service in July 1937 it was transferred to Gorgie during the war, then back to Leith after closure of that depot. The advert for 'Westons' biscuits was the very first 'paid' advert and appeared on a considerable number of buses and trams. (It even featured in the 'Scotsman' as the unacceptable face of commercialisation on the Corporation's vehicles.)

153. Waiting at the north Granton crossover is car 48. Fresh from Shrubhill in February 1950, one of the final six produced that year. Some of these cars had the ventilation strip above the lower deck windows painted in a lighter brown than usual. As one of the newest cars it was still extant in November 1956, and was used in the final procession on the 16th of that month, being the eighth last car into Shrubhill. It survived there for a further two months, not taken for scrap until 8 January the following year.

154. Car 50 in classic pose in the sun at foot of Craighall Road, where there were frequently lengthy stopovers resulting sometimes in an accumulation of cars. In use up to the last night, 50 went for scrap on 19 December 1956 after only six years of use. Dundee Corporation Tramways had enquired about purchase of some of these, but when they did, none were surplus. By 1956 the Dundee tramways were also doomed to imminent closure.

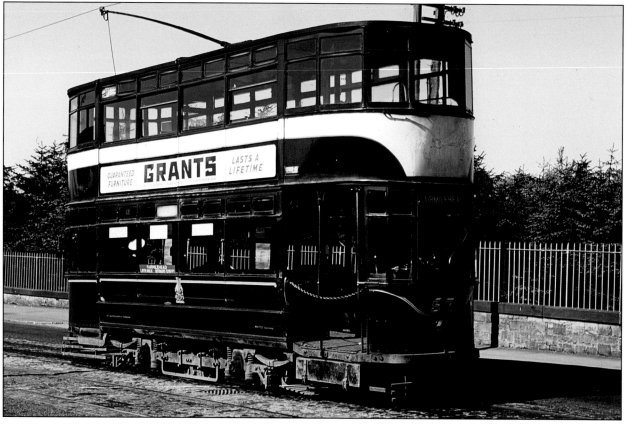

155. Fairmilehead terminus with car 57 built in June 1928. Unusually for Edinburgh's fleet it was not allocated permanently to one depot but was hawked around from Shrubhill to Gorgie to Leith to Tollcross and then finally back to Leith. Was there a particular problem with it? Whatever the reason it was in use until November 1955.

156. Foot of the Mound view of car 59 on service 23 to Morningside Station. In service from January 1947 to November 1956. Originally allocated to Portobello Depot when built, it was transferred to Tollcross when the former was closed.

157. At Fairmilehead terminus in the summer of 1955, is standard car 73. In service in July 1947, it was still in use at the end of the system's life. On 12 December 1956 it was removed from Shrubhill for scrapping in Coatbridge. The 'Evening Dispatch' advertised on the tram was Edinburgh's other evening paper, closed in 1963.

158. On 10 April 1955 car 91 on a special working turns down the seldom-used junction from York Place into Broughton Street. Built in May 1937 it was a Leith Depot car until transferred to Portobello in 1941 in exchange for the six streamlined type cars returned. This junction was used only on the infrequent occasions when processions or such like from Waterloo Place to Princes Street resulted in service 9 cars operating via York Place and terminating at St. Andrew Square.

159. Car 105 was one of the early cars of this style, out-shopped from Shrubhill Works in December 1935. It was a Portobello Depot car (a regular performer on route 5) until that depot closed in November 1954. Transferred to Leith it did not last till the final day, being despatched to Connell's during September 1956. Note the temporary crowd barriers at the kerb.

160. Granton terminus with cars 119 and 27. The former was built at Shrubhill in April 1931, one of the final developments of the 'wooden' style cars. This design was built without 'balcony' doors, the stair being enclosed in a 'cupboard'. The car was constructed with enclosed balconies both upstairs and below, indicated by the differing window arrangement from car 132 below. It went for scrap in November 1955.

The firm of McHardy & Elliot had its origins in the coming together of two coach building concerns. The earliest record of Charles M'Hardy is at Chapel Street Corstorphine and of Andrew Elliot in West Nicholson Street. The latter, as sole proprietor, registered the concern as a Limited Company in May 1920, in order to finance a move to larger premises following a rapid increase in business. The company then built 52 tramcar top decks for cable car modernisation, and 16 lower decks for electric trams. They were described as 'Coach and Motor Body Builders' with the telegraphic address 'Saloon'. Perhaps the move was not such a good one, as in mid-1924 the firm was wound up following a petition by creditors.

161. Car 132 is one of the batch first built for electrification of the Edinburgh system and is generally ascribed to McHardy & Elliot, but the top deck was by Hurst Nelson of Motherwell. They were also among the first cars to be scrapped, in 1949-52. This car, seen near Comely Bank terminus, is unusual in having no Corporation crest on the waist panel.

162. At Granton car 148 poses under a blue sky (it was NOT always thus!). One of the last of the old 'wooden' design, appearing in April 1934, it was individual, having upgraded saloon lighting. It was just two years younger than car 180, showing the vast advancement in design achieved in that short period. It was scrapped in December 1955. Independent brewers T. & J. Bernard owned Slateford brewery, but was closed down after acquisition by Scottish Brewers in 1960.

163. At the Lower Granton Road timing point for route 13, car 158 waits its allotted departure time. Completed in November 1931, it had a lower saloon wider than its predecessors, was one of only three cars which when built had non-standard triangular service colour lights. The top deck incorporated parts from former cable car top deck (as did many of the cars constructed up to this time at Shrubhill). Sold to Connell for scrap in April 1956. Note the beer advert. Another of Edinburgh's long disappeared local brewers, Wm. Murray's Craigmillar brewery closed in 1963 after purchase by Northern Breweries.

164. Also at Granton is car 167, portrayed here. Constructed in 1931 to the final design of 'wooden standard' car which was constructed without upper deck bulkheads. Note also the panel divisions to the upper deck ends, which were a feature of this stage of development.

165. The second last car built in Edinburgh, 172 appeared in July 1950, destined for revenue-earning service of just over six years. It was selected for decoration and was taken out of service in September 1956 for the design to be applied. As the 'Last Tram Week' car it toured the system and then took part in the final night procession. It went off on the one-way trip to Connells before the end of November that year.

166. Car 180 created quite a sensation when unveiled to the Transport Committee on 23 March 1932. The seemingly scandalous amount of £4,000 had been expended on this, the ultimate in lightweight tram design. (This equates to only some £120,000 in today's (year 2001) terms, when a new bus can cost up to £200,000.) It was painted pillar-box red until its first repaint in May 1935, but never lost its nickname 'Red Biddy'. Seen at the west end of Stanley Road, its historic significance must have been appreciated by somebody in the corridors of power, as it was the only non-standard tram which was allowed to remain in service until closure.

167. Granton Square with 201 on service 9 about to reverse on the mid-crossover of the three there. Built in June 1930 it ran from Leith Depot until withdrawn in April 1956. Note the window detailing with the top deck windows changed from wooden to metal framed.

168. Despite car 202 being one of the earliest '1934 – standard' cars (built March 1935), it was still in service at the end of operations but did not take part in the final procession. Seen at Belhaven Terrace, terminus of route 23 (and the earlier abandoned route 5).

169. Car 215 at Fairmilehead terminus. Built in July 1939 it was one of the final operational cars. Always operated from Leith Depot it was in use up to the final day. Despatched to Connell of Coatbridge for scrap on 20 November 1956.

170. Looking north at Fairmilehead terminus, with car 217 on service 16 for Bernard Street, a working which dates the view to before mid-June 1956. Thereafter the 16 was extended to Granton.

171. Front end contrasts at Granton, with cars 222 and 18 apparently about to set off on a race! 222 dated from January 1939 and ran until the end. It left Shrubhill for scrap the day before 217 above, 19 November 1956.

172. Car 234 at the favourite site for photography at Granton. It is on service 9 to Colinton, and is about to reverse over the middle crossover to commence its journey. The service colour box should show yellow/yellow.

173. Car 237 heading east on Princes Street on the outer Marchmont Circle service. The ventilator strip on this car is darker than average. 237, built December 1936, was despatched from Shrubhill for scrap on 27 August 1956.

174. Car 238 at Granton Square crossover on route 10 to Colinton. In service in January 1937, it ran from Tollcross Depot for most of its existence. Note the side board stuck behind the seat back below the side destination box. In 1954 services 10 and 16 were altered, thus the side destination screen was inaccurate. Rather than change these, side boards were carried instead. Sent to Connells on 19 October 1956.

175. Car 239 at Granton. One of three (231,239 and 240) similar cars built by Hurst Nelson & Co of Motherwell, the design incorporated many new features. They were of steel construction, not perpetuated in the 1934 style of locally-built car. Notwithstanding its peculiarities it remained in use until April 1956.

176. Braids terminus 1956 with car 247 on route 28. The conductress is returning to the car after reversing the trolley. The side destination screen prior to 1954 related to service 16, but is correct in 1956 for service 28. Always a Leith Depot car, it ran from March 1937 to the end of August 1956.

177. The ten cars from R. Y. Pickering of Wishaw were delivered between the end of 1932 and the start of the following year. Unusually they were given consecutive numbers – formerly occupied by withdrawn ex-Leith open top cars. They had some novel features when new – such as headlamps and windscreen wipers. 256 of this batch in Princes Street shows the 'double mullion' arrangement at the route number/colour light box.

178. In its final months of operation, and looking slightly the worse for wear, 260 was photographed in Princes Street. In service in February 1933, and based all its days at Leith Depot, it went for scrap in early July 1956.

179. The 'odd' contractor-built cars of 1933 occupied fleet numbers vacated by former Leith cars scrapped at this time. 260 was an all-metal bodied variety of the 180 design, built by Metropolitan-Cammel. In appearance they differed from 180 with angular end panels and flat glass in lieu of curved (expensive!) glass of 180. Note also that the roof edge trim on these cars was red, (180 was black). Seen in 1951 on the track fan of Leith Depot.

180. 'One-off' car 261 was brought out from Shrubhill works in September 1933. Very much a prototype for the standard car of the following year it had a more conventional appearance. Again, a transitional design, not perpetuated, but which never the less was operated with basically standard equipment.

181. Lower Granton Road view of car 262, one of the three prototype 'streamline' style cars supplied by English Electric. The 'raked' ends of these cars resulted in a reduction in top deck seating of two passengers! Again, like most of these 'non-standard' cars it spent all its days working from Leith Depot. Some of the windows seem to be falling out of their frames. It was sent for scrap on 19 April 1956. Note the large railway water tank behind.

182. While similar in appearance to the ten 'Pickerings', 264 was in fact built by the Corporation in July 1931. It ran from Leith until sent for scrap in December 1955. For its first year it ran on a Maley & Taunton 'swing-link' truck which was transferred to 'Red Biddy' 180 in April 1932. By the time of this photograph all non-standard trucks had disappeared and 264 is on the 'regulation' Peckham style.

183. Car 265 at Granton Square terminus, the second of the two non standard flat-roofed cars built by Metropolitan-Cammel in 1933. It assumed, in 1953, a unique identity as the only tram to carry the advertisement seen here for 'Jack's Locker' – a fish and chip establishment in Bath Street Portobello!

184. Busy scene in Princes Street at Hanover Street with, nearest to the camera, car 280, one of fifty-four supplied by the Leeds Forge Company's Bristol works in 1923 for the electrification programme. The Leeds Forge, better known as builders of railway wagons, had then recently acquired the Bristol Wagon & Carriage Works Coy. These were the only tramcars constructed by them, the Bristol end of the organisation being closed the following year. Car 280 went for scrap on 6 August 1954.

PASSENGERS
ARE REQUESTED
TO SIT FACING
DIRECTION CAR
IS TRAVELLING.

185. Stanley Road (west end) with car 353 constructed by Shrubhill works in November 1926. On this car the upper deck balcony ends were open when built, being enclosed in May 1931 with the top deck bulkheads being retained. It was normally a Leith Depot car, remaining in use until February 1955.

186. Princes Street view of car 362 which dated from October 1929. One of the last to be constructed with open ends to the top deck, it ran in this condition for less than a year, becoming totally enclosed in July 1930. For most of its life it operated from Portobello Depot but was transferred when it closed to Leith for its last year until scrapped in November 1955.

187. Cars 363 and 364 (below) were both former stalwarts of the Joppa and Levenhall route but ran their last months on services operated from Leith Depot. Both dated from November 1929, and were given enclosed top decks, in 1932/3. 363 was scrapped in November 1955 its sister five months later.

188. Car 364 is also seen at Granton during its last few months of service. The layout of the advertisements on the two cars is remarkably similar. A panel decided suitability of adverts for Edinburgh trams, but there does seem to be a remarkable lack of originality here. Initially alcoholic beverage adverts were not deemed acceptable, until economic sense prevailed.

189. The ex-Manchester Corporation 'Pilcher' cars purchased in 1947-49 were not considered a particularly good buy. Although they cost only £210 each (equivalent to c.£4,000 today) they were in poor condition and required considerable re-vamping before being put in service. However they were necessary at the time and deemed a short-term expedient. They differed in several respects from the 'norm', one unique feature being the enclosure of the stairs (to prevent draughts) by a folding 'trap door' level with the top deck floor. Car 405 (former Manchester 558), in service in 1949, went for scrap on 26 April 1954.

190. From March 1953 until July 1954 cars for scrap were uplifted from Corstorphine terminus. Here an unidentified former Manchester car starts on its last ignominious journey. Why Connell found it necessary to transport the cars to their yard in Coatbridge for scrapping is open to question. Could not the use of some closer premises – a former depot for example – have saved the transport cost? These cars never carried side adverts on the upper deck panels.

191. When Edinburgh's tramways were electrified in the 1920's, the benefits of motor traction for 'works' duties had been realised, hence there was no large fleet of, for example, 'sand and set' cars as in Glasgow. Nevertheless ten cars were in use for departmental purposes when the system was at its peak. By 1955 only two remained. The most surprising survivor was rail grinder car 1, which was by far the oldest car in the fleet, having started life in 1905 as Leith Corporation's water/snowplough car. How much of the original was left is open to conjecture. It was never officially scrapped but disintegrated over the years in a quiet corner of Shrubhill.

192. The only works car extant in 1956 was rail grinder 3. Its saloon started life as cable car 51, built by the Edinburgh District Co. in 1908. Electrified in 1923, it ran in passenger service until 1942. Seen here in North St Andrew Street on 16 November 1956, last day of operation. It has the unique distinction for that day of flying pennants on its trolley rope. It mouldered in Shrubhill until early 1957 – why could it not have been tucked in a corner and forgotten – the only surviving former cable car?

APPENDIX 1

SERVICES & PARCELS

TRAMWAY ROUTES

Service No.	ROUTE	Route Colour	Service No.	ROUTE	Route Colour
1	Liberton and Corstorphine	Red Blue	15	Braids and King's Road via York Place and London Road	Green White
2	Granton and Stenhouse via York Place and George Street	Blue	16	Fairmilehead and Granton Square via York Pl., Leith Walk & Junction St.	Green
3	Newington Stn. and Stenhouse via Princes Street	Blue White	17	Newington Stn. & Granton Square via Bernard Street	White
4	Piershill and Slateford via London Road and Princes Street	White Blue	19	Craigentinny Ave. No. & Tollcross via Bridges and Melville Drive	Green Red
5	Morningside Stn., Salisbury and Piershill via Grange Road and Bridges	Red Green	20	Edinburgh G.P.O., Portobello and Joppa	Red
6	Marchmont Circle (Either Direction) P.O., Marchmont, West End	White Red	21	Edinburgh G.P.O., Portobello, Musselburgh and Levenhall	Green
7	Liberton and Stanley Road via Junction Street	Red	23	Granton Rd. Stn., Tollcross, Bruntsfield & Morningside via Mound	Green Yellow
8	Granton Sq. and Newington Stn. via Broughton St.	Red Yellow	24	Waverley, Stockbridge and Comely Bank via Frederick Street	Red
9	Granton Square and Colinton via Broughton St.	Yellow	25	Drum Brae South and King's Road via York Place and Leith Walk	Blue Yellow
10	Bernard Street and Colinton	White Yellow	26	Piershill and Drum Brae South via London Road and Princes Street	Blue Red
11	Fairmilehead and Stanley Road via Pilrig Street	Red White	27	Granton Rd. Stn., and Firrhill via Mound and Lauriston	Yellow Red
12	Corstorphine, King's Road and Joppa via Leith & Seafield	Yellow Blue	28	Braids and Stanley Road via Pilrig Street	Blue Green
13	Churchhill and Granton Circle via Pilrig Street	White Green			
14	Churchhill and Granton Circle via Bernard Street	Yellow Green			

Missing from this 1951 official list are services 18 and 22. The 18, Liberton Dams to Waverley via Melville Drive had been replaced by buses in March 1950. Its route colours were yellow/white. The original 22, GPO to Port Seton, ceased in 1928 but the number and colour (blue/blue) were retained for a short working of service 21 operating as far as Musselburgh Town Hall, but this fell out of use in c.1943. The number and colour were reinstated from October 1946 for a similar part day and part route operation on service 2, from Stenhouse to North Junction Street only. It is interesting to note that late night 2 cars often ran by way of Princes Street instead of George Street – it being reasoned that there was more traffic to be gained on the former busier street.

Enamelled sign displayed by agents for the Parcels Service.

CITY OF EDINBURGH TRANSPORT DEPARTMENT

PARCELS DELIVERY SERVICE

Speedy delivery to all parts of the City by Motor Vans
Parcels accepted by Tramway Car and Motor Bus Conductors

Parcel Tickets can be obtained from the Transport Offices, 2 St. James' Square, and the following District Agents :—

R. Forrest, I Antigua Street
D. Henderson, 54 Elm Row
M. Oxley, 32 Crighton Place
M.'Heatly, 149 Leith Walk
A. Aitken, 2 Leith Walk
J. Groves, 58 Bernard Street
J. Durrand, 15 Portland Place
R. Ratter, 80 Main Street, Newhaven
E. Edwards, 40 Lower Granton Road
T. T. Wood, 96 Newhaven Road

Mrs McDonald, 48 George IV Bridge
Gardner Bros., 14 Teviot Place
A. B. Fleming, 51 Nicholson Street
Geo. Geddes, 32 South Clerk Street
A. Walker Gibb, 3 Salisbury Place
M. Robinson, Braefoot, Liberton
F. McLachlan, Liberton Gardens

W. Renton, 123 Dalry Road
Fernies of Dalry, 259 Dalry Road
A. Foulis, 61 Slateford Road
E. & B. Harris, 560 Gorgie Road
Albert Whyte, Post Office, Sighthill
Mrs Porteous, Juniper Green

E. & M Chalmers, 65 Broughton Street
Jas. McCulloch, 91 Pitt Street
Geo. McDonald, 3 Howard Street
D. Robertson, 28 Montague Terrace
G. L. White, 6 Inverleith Gardens
D. Ewart, 230 Crewe Road, N.
A. Watson, 157 Granton Road

A. Scott, 75 Lothian Road
Flemings' Stores, Earl Grey Street
D. Henderson, 31 Home Street
A. & J. Whittaker, 25 Marchmont Crescent
A. D. Hunter, 81 Bruntsfield Place
J. C. Smith, 9 Churchill Place
M. & J. Pinkerton, 382 Morningside Road

Guthrie & Co., (Scot.) Ltd., 9a West Maitland Street
A. D. McKenzie, 69 Haymarket Terrace
H. T. Mitchell, 4 Roseburn Terrace
F. Weierter & Son, 172 St. John's Road, Corstorphine

A. Aitken, 12 Polwarth Gardens
J. Riley, 118 Colinton Road
Waddell Bros., Colinton

E. Gilchrist, 32 Howe Street
K. A. McIvor, 7 Kerr Street, Stockbridge
J. Borthwick, 6 Craigleith Road

G. C. Bryce, 78 Montrose Terrace
C. & I. Russell, 9 Meadowbank Terrace
Albert Whyte, 100 Northfield Broadway
R. C. Hutcheson, 149 High Street, Portobello
D. Wilson, 23 Morton Street, Joppa
L. Leask, 2 Restalrig Road

Durie Brown, 21 Queensferry Street
J. D. Henderson, 18 W. Barnton Terrace
W. J. & C. D. Reynolds, Main Street, Davidson's Mains
Mrs Wilson, 7 Almond Bank, Cramond

Parcels Receiving and Delivery Office : I Shrub Place
'phone—Cen. 2784.

APPENDIX 2
CABLE TRAMS

Relics of the cable car period in Edinburgh's transport are few. This delightful large-scale model of cable tram 81 was, it is believed, for use in a Court case. Only missing its top deck seating, it was regularly displayed during the Infirmary pageants of the 1930's, and then in the Transport Department's museum.

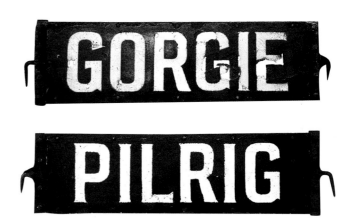

Destination signs as hung from the ends of cable trams.

Edinburgh's first cable tramcar ran on 28 January 1888, the last on 23 June 1923. The highly complex system of continuously moving underground cables was a marvel of Victorian ingenuity. Basically a fine idea to overcome traction problems on the City's many hills; eventually over 200 trams operated on 25 miles of track.

APPENDIX 3
HORSE TRAMS

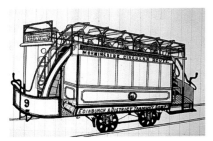  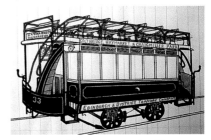

'Naïve', but surprisingly accurate, drawings of the route colours used on Edinburgh's horse tramways. These are contained in a notebook handed in to the Transport Dept's former Queen Street offices some years ago. White liveried car 9 is for the Morningside Circle; 16 is red and white for Bernard Street to North Merchiston; 33 is dark brown and white for Coltbridge to Craigmillar Park.

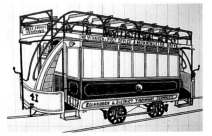 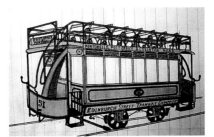 

On the second row car 41 is 'Oak' and white for Newhaven to Morningside Drive; 51 is yellow for Portobello to Colinton Road, and 74 (a second-hand Glasgow car) is 'chocolate and buff' for Coltbridge to Powburn.

On the third row car 82 is blue and white for Commercial Street to Marchmont Road; 101 (another ex-Glasgow) is 'ochre' and white for Tron Church to Tollcross; and knifeboard seat car 110 is green and buff, operating Seafield to Gorgie Road. Differentiation of routes by colour was introduced in April 1883 by J Clifton Robinson while he was Manager of the Edinburgh Street Tramway Company. Coloured lights for night time were introduced at the same time ... the probable basis for their use in electric car days.

Like many cities, Edinburgh built horse tramways as a great improvement on earlier horse buses. From a start in November 1871 the system expanded to a maximum of over 100 cars on 19 miles of route. Operated by a private company leasing tracks owned by the local authority, the original lease existed until 1894 when operations were split in two, with tramways in the district Burgh of Leith being operated separately (but by the original lessee). The new operator of the tramways within Edinburgh formed a new company, the Edinburgh District Tramways Co., to gradually reconstruct for cable operation, the last horse car running on 24 August 1907. In Leith the Corporation ran the horse trams from 23 October 1904, then proceeded to electrify and operate them, until the Burgh was amalgamated with Edinburgh on 20 November 1920.

THE FUTURE?

193 Munich 2001

194 Croydon 2001

Today, some forty-five years after closure of the Edinburgh tram system, the modern tram provides rapid urban transit in over 350 locations throughout the world. Over 60 of these are completely new operations. Europe and the former Soviet Union never lost faith, but to combat growing pollution and traffic overload, new systems have been built – and more are proposed – for Europe, North America and Japan.

The upper view opposite shows a modern tram in Edinburgh's initial 'twin' city, Munich, in Germany. Here, in the nineteen-fifties trams were retained, the suburban railways electrified and in the seventies an underground rail system was constructed. The trams were modernised and the parts moulded together to provide an integrated and efficient urban transport solution. Modern trams serve both city centre streets and the suburbs adding to the quality of life.

Four English cities have, over the last ten years, introduced new light rail transit systems. Illustrated (lower opposite) is the most recent of these, in Croydon, south of London opened in the year 2000. Four lines radiate to suburbs, with extensions already proposed. The new form of transport is popular and the system is already well used, with retailers reporting an upsurge in business.

In Edinburgh during the last twenty-five years light rail reintroduction has been proposed, but "in the long term". Commissioning of numerous studies by the local authority have produced little tangible improvement. So far only piecemeal, low cost schemes have been implemented – green paint on roads for bus priority routes, and a 'guided bus' proposal which has yet failed to materialise. It is considered that these minor changes have failed to alleviate the pollution, noise and traffic overload in the streets of Scotland's capital city. At times Princes Street has become a continuous line of stationary, pollution-creating, oil-driven, de-regulated buses. In the meantime other cities in Europe, North America – and indeed England –are able to invest the large sums necessary for rail and light rail projects. The debate in Edinburgh rumbles on, but it seems inevitable that funding – from both government and private sectors – must be made available in the near future. The City of Edinburgh Council's vision of a light rail urban transport solution needs to be driven forward into a reality if the city is to solve its impending traffic crisis.

ONLINE VIDEO in co-operation with 226 Group and the Edinburgh Transport Group

EDINBURGH TRAMS

Trams from the Thirties – 3 car types at Fairmilehead on 31 July, 1955. Wood Standard no. 31 (1930); Shrubhill Standard 165 (1935) and 180 the experimental 'Red Biddy' of 1932. W. G. S. Hyde.

Edinburgh occupies a unique place in the history of British tramways. Horse cars were operated from 1871-1907; cable trams (the fifth largest system in the world) from 1888-1923; but electric trams did not arrive until 1922 except for a line in Musselburgh (1904); Leith, then an independent burgh (1905); and a short line to Slateford (1910). Extensions were built until 1937 and new trams emerged from Shrubhill works until 1950. The first service was replaced by buses in 1950, with the last trams operating on 16 November, 1956.

This tape recaptures the time when trams dominated the city. Also featured – vintage vehicles inc. buses and trains, street furniture, fashions, shops, streets and scenes long since disappeared.

A FEAST OF MEMORIES.

Help preserve the city's tramway heritage – buy the highly acclaimed ONLINE VIDEO

EDINBURGH TRAMS

Superb atmospheric sequences including much in COLOUR. Magnificent pre-war sequences; depot & works scenes; rugby specials; works cars; all major city streets; coloured route lights; most car types in action inc. 'Manchesters'; detailed coverage of route closures 1954-56; stunning last day activity. A feast of memories. Also rich in contemporary buses, cars, street furniture etc.

Two hours of sheer nostalgia for just £19.00 (inc p/p)

To ensure profits go towards preserving Edinburgh 226 order from/cheques payable to The 226 Fund, 8 Dalhousie Terrrace, Edinburgh EH10 5NE.

'excellent value' – Tramway & Urban Transit

If you have enjoyed this book, perhaps you would like to read the following publications about the Edinburgh trams:

Edinburgh's Transport. Volume 2 – The Corporation Years, 1919-1975

D.L.G. Hunter. Edited by Alan Brotchie and Alastair Gunn. Softback, 192 pages, £20.
Contents: Introduction; The New Corporation Transport Department; Electrification and the End of the Cable System; Consolidation and Expansion; Under New Management; Robert McLeod in Charge; Wartime Operations; Postwar Changes and the Decline of the Tram; The Bus Omnipotent; The Regional Regime; plus Appendices on – Tramcars; Rolling Stock; Buses; Tickets; Statistics. Over 150 illustrations.
    "...an extremely detailed volume with a fine selection of beautifully produced pictures ... there is a lot here for your £20. Excellent." [Archive]

Edinburgh Street Tramways Company Rules and Regulations for the Servants

1883, 56pp, limited edition, softback, £8.

Source book of Literature Relating to Scottish tramways

48pp. D.Croft & A.Gordon, softback, £5.

and for other books of Scottish interest:

and a selection of other titles:

The Twilight Years of the Glasgow Tram

First in the series of "Twilight Years". Softback, 144 pages, £25.
Contains over 250 coloured pictures taken by Douglas McMillan, selected, prefaced and captioned by Alasdair Turnbull, who has maintained a humorous and homely commentary on a clockwise tour of the Glasgow system as it was in the 1950's and early 1960's. Published to celebrate the centenary of the introduction of electric traction to the Glasgow tramways on 13th October 1898.
    "Every so often one comes across a book which is almost beyond compare, and this is one such. More, it is sure to set a new standard for albums, and one to which every author and publisher might do well to aspire...a wonderful book..." [Tramway Museum Society Journal]

The Wearing of the Green

William Tollan. Softback, A4 size, 96 pages, 64 pages in mono, 16 pages in colour; covers coloured on both sides, £12.
This describes the Glasgow tramways from c.1928-1951 from the viewpoint of a driver and conductor. "I think this is the most fascinating and amusing book on trams I have ever read." [Publisher]
    "This is a dangerous book. Dangerous because once you pick it up you will find it impossible to put down until the end! ... Excellent value for money and thoroughly recommended." [Industrial Heritage]
    "This book is well laid out and the pictures are crisply reproduced ... well worth reading by anyone who likes the social side rather than the history and minutiae." [Archive]

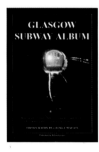

Glasgow Subway Album

G. Watson. All colour paperback, 64pp, £10.
"What is amazing about this volume is the quality of the photographs, for almost all were taken under artificial lighting ... portraying the system much as the human eye would see it ... This is a superb production covering a little-known railway, and does its job very well indeed." [TMS Journal] "The pictures reflect the day-to-day life on the line and as such proves to be a superb record of the only other subway line in the UK other than London Transport. With 115 colour pictures the volume is excellent value." [Tramfare]

Clippie

Z.Katin, a few months in the life of a tram and bus conductress in the war in Sheffield, 124pp, softback, reprint, £7

The Douglas Horse Tramway

Keith Pearson. Softback, A4 size, 96 pages, coloured covers, and over 135 illustrations. £14.50

"Double Century"

Stan Basnett and Keith Pearson. 144 pages, including 8 in colour, and numerous illustrations. Hardbacked in red buckrum with gold lettering. £15.
It comprises updated histories of the Upper Douglas Cable Tramway, and the Douglas Head Marine Drive Tramway. It also includes an appendix on the Cliff Lifts. Ch.4 consists of 'guided walks' along the routes today by Stan Basnett.

The History of the Steam Tram

H.A. Whitcombe. Hardback, 88pp, £12.00

How to go Tram and Tramway Modelling

David Voice. Softback, with coloured covers, 168 pages, 150 black & white photographs, 34 diagrams, and an illustrated glossary. £15

London County Council Tramways Guide to Reopening of Kingsway Subway

Reprint of 1931 publication, coloured cover and map, 32pp, softback, £6

My Life in Many States and in Foreign Lands

G.F.Train. reprint of autobiography of street railway pioneer, originally published in 1902; over 350pp, softback, £12

Tramways and Electric Railways in the Nineteenth Century

(Electric Railway Number of Cassier's Magazine, 1899), cloth hardback, over 250pp, £23

Tramways – Their Construction and Working

D.K.Clark. 2nd edn of 1894, over 750pp, 12 plates and over 400 line drawings, cloth hardback, £32

The Definitive Guide to Trams and Funiculars in The British Isles

David Voice. Softback, 182pp, 72 photos, coloured covers, £15
Updated and greatly expanded version of The Millennium Guide to Trams. "...a good reliable guide ... A very handy little volume indeed, worth every penny." [TMS Journal]

Postage and packing on new books, UK retail: please add 10% of the value of the order up to £4.90 maximum. Orders £50 and over post free. Overseas postage extra, at cost. Overseas payments must please be by cheque, drawn on a British bank, and payable in Sterling.

ADAM GORDON, Priory Cottage, Chetwode, Buckingham MK18 4LB. Tel: 01280 848650